LifeLight

"In Him was life, and the life was the light of men." John 1:4

Heaven and Hell

LEADERS GUIDE

CONCORDIA PUBLISHING HOUSE • SAINT LOUIS

We will see that the word *heaven* hardly does justice to the glory of life in the age to come. Perhaps the voice that John heard from heaven says it best: "Behold, the dwelling place of God is with man. He will dwell with them, and they will be His people, and God Himself will be with them as their God" (Revelation 21:3). After the resurrection, believers will not be in heaven. Heaven will be with us.

Art excerpt from *John on Island of Patmos*
© CPH/Arthur Kirchhoff

Copyright © 2012 Concordia Publishing House
3558 S. Jefferson Ave., St. Louis, MO 63118-3968
1-800-325-3040 • www.cph.org

Written by David Loy

Edited by Brian Chisamore

Field testing coordinated by Rev. Eric Van Scyoc, St. Thomas Lutheran Church, Rocky River, OH

Cover illustration by © CPH/Arthur Kirchhoff

This publication may be available in Braille, in large print, or on cassette tape for the visually impaired. Please allow 8 to 12 weeks for delivery. Write to Lutheran Blind Mission, 7550 Watson Rd., St. Louis, MO 63119-4409; call toll-free 1-888-215-2455; or visit the Web site: www .blindmission.org.

Manufactured in the United States of America

1 2 3 4 5 6 7 8 9 10 21 20 19 18 17 16 15 14 13 12

Contents

Introduction

Welcome to LifeLight

A special pleasure is in store for you. You will be instrumental in leading your brothers and sisters in Christ closer to Him who is our life and light (John 1:4). You will have the pleasure of seeing fellow Christians discover new insights and rediscover old ones as they open the Scriptures and dig deep into them, perhaps deeper than they have ever dug before. More than that, you will have the pleasure of sharing in this wonderful study.

LifeLight—An In-depth Study

LifeLight is a series of in-depth Bible studies. The goal of LifeLight is that through a regular program of in-depth personal and group study of Scripture, more and more Christian adults may grow in their personal faith in Jesus Christ, enjoy fellowship with the members of His body, and reach out in love to others in witness and service.

In-depth means that this Bible study includes the following four components: individual daily home study; discussion in a small group; a lecture presentation on the Scripture portion under study; and an enhancement of the week's material (through reading the enrichment magazine).

LifeLight Participants

LifeLight participants are adults who desire a deeper study of the Scriptures than is available in the typical Sunday morning adult Bible class. (Mid-to-older teens might also be LifeLight participants.) While LifeLight does not assume an existing knowledge of the Bible or special experience or skills in Bible study, it does assume a level of commitment that will bring participants to each of the nine weekly assemblies having read the assigned readings and attempted to answer the study questions. Daily reading and study will require from 15 to 30 minutes for the five days preceding the LifeLight assembly. The day following the assembly will be spent reviewing the previous week's study by going over the completed study leaflet and the enrichment magazine.

LifeLight Leadership

While the in-depth process used by LifeLight begins with individual study and cannot achieve its aims without this individual effort, it cannot be completed by individual study alone. Therefore, trained leaders are necessary. You fill one or perhaps more of the important roles described below.

The Director

This person oversees the LifeLight program in a local center (which may be a congregation or a center operated by several neighboring congregations). The director

- serves as the parish LifeLight overall coordinator and leader;
- coordinates the scheduling of the LifeLight program;
- orders materials;
- convenes LifeLight leadership-team meetings;
- develops publicity materials;
- recruits participants;
- maintains records and budgeting;
- assigns, with the leadership-team, participants to small discussion groups;
- makes arrangements for facilities;
- communicates outreach opportunities to small-group leaders and to congregational boards;
- follows up on participants who leave the program.

The Assistant Director *(optional)*

This person may assist the director. Duties listed for the director may be assigned to the assistant director as mutually agreeable.

The Lecture Leader

This person prepares and delivers the lecture at the weekly assembly. **(Lesson material for the lecture leader begins on p. 9.)** The lecture leader

- prepares and presents the Bible study lecture to the large group;

- prepares worship activities (devotional thought, hymn, prayer), using resources in the study leaflet and leaders guide and possibly other, outside sources;
- helps the small-group discussion leaders to grow in understanding the content of the lessons;
- encourages prayer at weekly leadership-team and discussion leaders meetings.

The Small-Group Coordinator *(optional; the director may fill this role)*

This person supervises and coordinates the work of the small-group discussion leaders. The small-group coordinator

- recruits with the leadership-team the small-group discussion leaders;
- trains or arranges for training of the discussion leaders;
- assists the director and discussion leaders in follow-up and outreach;
- encourages the discussion leaders to contact absent group members;
- participates in the weekly leadership-team and discussion-leaders equipping meetings;
- provides ongoing training and support as needed. **The Small-Group Discussion Leaders**

These people guide and facilitate discussion of LifeLight participants in the small groups. **(Lesson material for the small-group leaders begins on p. 57.)** There should be one discussion leader for every group of no more than twelve participants. The small-group discussion leaders are, perhaps, those individuals who are most important to the success of the program. They should, therefore, be chosen with special care and be equipped with skills needed to guide discussion and to foster a caring fellowship within the group. These discussion leaders

- prepare each week for the small-group discussion by using the study leaflet and small-group leaders guide section for that session **(see p. 57)**;
- read the enrichment magazine as a study supplement;
- guide and facilitate discussion in their small group;
- encourage and assist the discussion group in prayer;
- foster fellowship and mutual care within the discussion group;
- attend weekly discussion leaders training meetings.

Leadership Training

LifeLight leaders will meet weekly to review the previous week's work and plan the coming week. At this session, leaders can address concerns and prepare for the coming session. LifeLight is a 1½-hour program with no possibility for it to be taught in the one hour typically available on Sunday mornings. Some congregations, however, may want to use the Sunday morning Bible study hour for LifeLight preparation and leadership training. In such a meeting, the lecture leader and/or small-group coordinator may lead the discussion leaders through the coming week's lesson, reserving 5 or 10 minutes for problem solving or other group concerns.

While it requires intense effort, LifeLight has proven to bring great benefit to LifeLight participants. The effort put into this program, both by leaders and by participants, will be rewarding and profitable.

The LifeLight Weekly Schedule

Here is how LifeLight will work week by week:

1. Before session 1, each participant will receive the study leaflet for session 1 and the enrichment magazine for the course. The study leaflet contains worship resources (for use both in individual daily study and at the opening of the following week's assembly) and readings and study questions for five days. Challenge questions will lead those participants who have the time and desire a greater challenge into even deeper levels of study.

2. After the five days of individual study at home, participants will gather for a weekly assembly of all LifeLight participants. The assembly will begin with a brief period of worship (5 minutes). Participants will then join their assigned small discussion groups (of twelve or fewer, who will remain the same throughout the course), where they will go over the week's study questions together (55 minutes). Assembling together once again, participants will listen to a lecture presentation on the readings they have studied in the previous week and discussed in their small groups (20 minutes). After the lecture presentation, the director or another leader will distribute the study leaflet for the following week.

Closing announcements and other necessary business may take another five minutes before dismissal.

In some places some small groups will not join the weekly assembly because of scheduling or other reasons. Such groups may meet at another time and place (perhaps in the home of one of the small group's members). Those congregations may record the lecture given by the lecture leader at the weekly assembly and duplicate it for use by other groups meeting later in the week.

3. On the day following the assembly, participants will review the preceding week's work by rereading the study leaflet they completed (and that they perhaps supplemented or corrected during the discussion in their small group) and by reading appropriate articles in the enrichment magazine.

Then the LifeLight weekly study process will begin all over again!

Recommended Study Resources and Worship

The Lutheran Study Bible. St. Louis: Concordia Publishing House, 2009. This resource contains more than 26,000 study and application notes, a most thorough reference guide (pp. lxv-cx), and over 90,000 cross-references, as well as a 31,000-entry concordance, maps, charts, and timelines.

Roehrs, Walter R., and Martin H. Franzmann. *Concordia Self-Study Commentary*. St. Louis: Concordia Publishing House, 1979. This one-volume commentary on the Bible contains 950 pages and is tailored for lay use.

The Concordia Organist is a 31-CD collection of pipe organ accompaniments for all the hymns and liturgical music in *Lutheran Service Book*. St. Louis: Concordia Publishing House (order no.99-2264). Use these CDs for worship hymn accompaniment.

A Guided Tour of Heaven and Hell

Selected Passages

Preparing for the Session

Central Focus

By nature, each of us deserves eternal punishment for rejecting God and misusing His gifts. Thankfully, His Son, Jesus, opened the door to heaven through His death and resurrection, so that believers can live with Him forever.

Objectives

That participants, led by the Holy Spirit working through God's Word, will

1. gain an overview of what happens to believers after death;
2. gain an overview of what happens to unbelievers after death; and
3. find comfort in God's gracious gift of heaven.

Note for the small-group leaders: Lesson notes and other materials you will need begin on page 57.

For the Lecture Leader

Session Plan

Worship

Begin the session with the hymn printed in the study leaflet. Accompaniments are available in denominational hymnals, such as *Lutheran Service Book* or *Lutheran Worship* (refer to hymnal index). (Note: Concordia Publishing House has available *The Concordia Organist*, a 31-CD collection of pipe organ accompaniments for all the hymns and liturgical music in *Lutheran Service Book*. All the initial worship hymns in the LifeLight courses are included in this resource. It's especially helpful for mission congregations and small parishes. See the list of study resources on p. 7.) Follow with this prayer:

Prayer

Almighty, everlasting God, Your Son has assured forgiveness of sins and deliverance from eternal death. Strengthen us by Your Holy Spirit that our faith in Christ may increase daily and that we may hold fast to the hope that on the Last Day we shall be raised in glory to eternal life; through Jesus Christ, our Lord. Amen. (*LSB Altar Book*, p. 453)

Lecture Presentation

Introduction

"Abandon all hope, all you who enter here." In the book-length poem *Inferno*, Italian poet Dante Alighieri describes how the Roman poet Virgil took him on a guided tour of hell. Dante sees these words inscribed above the gates of hell when they enter; as they work their way down the various levels of hell, they see horrible punishments meted out to sinners of every sort. Perhaps you have read the book, or at least heard of it. If not, don't worry. While the book and its sequels, *Purgatorio* and *Paradisio*, are classic literature, they are not the source of our true knowledge about heaven and hell. Our true knowledge about heaven and hell comes from a book you are more familiar with, and this LifeLight study will give you a guided tour of heaven and hell based on this book, the Bible.

Future sessions will examine various aspects of the doctrines of heaven and hell in depth—you can get an idea what topics will be covered by looking at the table of contents. For now, a quick tour of heaven and hell is in order, so that you can get a better picture of what the Bible says and how its various statements fit together. The fact is, heaven and hell are not simply places where people go, so to speak, depending on whether they believe in Jesus or not. Heaven and hell both have important places in God's plan of salvation. Heaven is His gift of grace to believers, where they will live forever in the presence of the One who has saved them, without any temptation or persecution by those who continue to reject God and His people. Hell is where those who do not look to God for salvation will get exactly what they want—eternity without the triune God. In the words of Daniel, (12:2–3) "Many of those who sleep in the dust of the earth shall awake, some to everlasting life, and some to shame and everlasting contempt. And those who are wise shall shine like the brightness of the sky above; and those who turn many to righteousness, like the stars forever and ever."

1 "In the Day That You Eat of It You Shall Surely Die"

Understanding heaven and hell requires that we first understand humanity, which in turn requires that we understand God. After all, (Genesis 1:27) "God created man in His own image, in the image of God He created him; male and female He created them." If we really are creatures—that is, created beings—then the God who created us has something to do with our fate. If, for example, the god who created us were a malicious god, he would simply hurt us in the worst possible way. That would be a god who would put everyone in hell simply for the sheer joy of it. Or, if the god who created us were an indifferent god, then he would leave us to our own devices. He might occasionally listen to our prayers and intervene to help us, but only if it suited his purposes. That would be a god who couldn't care less about having us around. Thankfully, the God who created us is neither of those things but, rather, is "a God merciful and gracious, slow to anger, and abounding in steadfast love and faithfulness" (Exodus 34:6). He holds us accountable for our sin, but through His Son, Jesus Christ, He also forgives our sin so that we can live in His presence forever.

Our God created us good. He blessed us and He gave us an entire earth to provide for us. When we fell into sin, He brought our sin to our attention, but He did so in order to point us to the promise of salvation through Him. To the serpent He said, (Genesis 3:15) "I will put enmity between you and the woman, and between your offspring and her offspring; He shall bruise your head, and you shall bruise His heel." Humanity fell to the power of the serpent, and unless someone more powerful than the serpent were to rescue us, we would remain under his power forever. Just after the fall, God promised a rescuer. He promised that one of Eve's offspring would disarm the serpent and rescue us from his power. This person would be fully human (seed of Eve) and yet have divine power (the power to defeat the serpent). You and I know this person as Jesus Christ. In Christ Jesus, we see a heavenly Father who both calls us on our sin and rescues us from our sin so that we can enjoy fellowship with Him. (1 John 1:8–9) "If we say we have no sin, we deceive ourselves, and the truth is not in us. If we confess our sins, He is faithful and just to forgive us our sins and to cleanse us from all unrighteousness."

From this, we learn a great deal about us human beings as well. We were created in God's image, and our ancestors Adam and Eve enjoyed an amazing fellowship with God at the beginning. God spoke with them. He walked in the garden with them. They lived in His presence. Then it all came apart. Eve ate of the fruit of the tree of the knowledge of good and evil, and her husband, Adam, who was with her, ate of the fruit as well. Their intent was quite innocent at first. The serpent went on and on about knowledge and good and evil and being like God, but ultimately Eve's motives were corrupted. (Genesis 3:6) "When the woman saw that the tree was good for food, and that it was a delight to the eyes, and that the tree was to be desired to make one wise, she took of its fruit and ate, and she also gave some to her husband who was with her." In general, if you are going to choose the fruit of some tree to eat, you would choose the fruit that is good for food, just as Eve did. No problem there. Generally speaking, you will choose the fruit that looks good and ripe, just as Eve did. No problem there. And as for seeking wisdom, well, that is good too. No problem there. In these respects, Eve's motives appear quite pure, according to the text. The problem was this: she disobeyed God. She ate of the fruit of the tree of which God had said, (Genesis 2:17) "You shall not eat, for in the day that you eat of it you shall surely die." Eve and her husband, Adam, had disobeyed God, and so they deserved death.

That is who you and I are—children of Adam and Eve, people who deserve death for the mere fact that we do not obey God. Motives do not matter. Even a person with entirely pure motives can disobey God, and that disobedience merits death. We are now creatures (created beings) who have walked away from the living words of the God who gave us life. We are wandering children of a loving God. Because we have sinned, we will die, and it is the topic of death that leads our thoughts to the topics of heaven and hell.

2 Do Believers Go to Heaven after They Die?

We are so used to saying that believers who die "go to heaven" that it may come as a surprise that the Scriptures do not use the phrase. The closest they come is in four places: 2 Kings 2:1; Matthew 11:23; Luke 10:15; and Revelation 11:12. In 2 Kings 2:1, the context is God's intent "to take Elijah up to heaven by a whirlwind." Of course, Elijah was not yet dead; the Lord had decided to take Elijah to heaven bodily. What exactly does the word *heaven* mean in the Old Testament? Throughout the Old Testament, the word *heaven* is used in two basic senses: (1) the sky (i.e., what we see when we look up, encompassing everything from flying birds to the clouds to the stars and planets) and (2) the place where God dwells. When we talk about a person's going to heaven, we are obviously interested in the second sense of the word.

Several passages shed light on what heaven in this sense means. Genesis 19:24, for example, tells us, "the LORD rained on Sodom and Gomorrah sulfur and fire from the LORD out of heaven." This is not simply fire from above; it is fire from the Lord out of heaven. In the same way, Genesis 21:17 tells us, "God heard the voice of the boy, and the angel of God called to Hagar from heaven and said to her, 'What troubles you, Hagar? Fear not, for God has heard the voice of the boy where he is.'" The angel of the Lord calls to Hagar from heaven. The Lord's instructions to the people in Deuteronomy 26:15 makes it clear that heaven is where God lives; He commands the people, when they bring their tithes, to pray, "Look down from Your holy habitation, from heaven, and bless Your people Israel and the ground that You have given us, as You swore to our fathers, a land flowing with milk and honey." Finally, Solomon's prayer of dedication for the temple calls again and again on the Lord to "hear in heaven" (1 Kings 8:32, 34, 36, 39). In other words, in the Old Testament, heaven is not so much a location where a person might arrive to find any number of other people coming or going. Heaven is, rather, where God lives. Heaven is less about a place and more about the person of God. When 2 Kings 2:1 says that God was preparing to take Elijah to heaven in a whirlwind, it is saying that God was preparing to take Elijah to Himself.

The New Testament understands heaven in the same way. Think about the introduction to the Lord's Prayer: "Our Father who art in heaven." Jesus refers to the Father in this way throughout the Gospel of Matthew: (5:16) "Let your light shine before others, so that they may see your good works and give glory to your Father who is in heaven." The Gospel of Luke is even more explicit. Speaking of the joy of the shepherd who finds the one sheep that went missing, Jesus says, (15:7) "Just so, I tell you, there will be more joy in heaven over one sinner who repents than over ninety-nine righteous persons who need no repentance." In the following parable, Jesus speaks of the joy of a woman who finds her lost coin, and then He says, (Luke 15:10) "Just so, I tell you, there is joy before the angels of God over one sinner who repents." Jesus' language here is careful. He does not say that the angels rejoice, but that there is more rejoicing "before the angels of God." Who could rejoice before the angels—that is, in the presence of the angels? None other than God Himself! So when Jesus says that there is more rejoicing in heaven over one sinner that repents than over one lost sheep who has been found, He is saying that God in heaven rejoices over repentant sinners. Finally, the Book of Hebrews says it explicitly: (8:1) "We have such a high priest, one who is seated at the right hand of the throne of the Majesty in heaven." And when Jesus was baptized, the Father's voice was heard "from heaven" (Matthew 3:17; Mark 1:11; Luke 3:22). Heaven is not a location on this earth to which you and I might journey. Heaven is where—or better said, wherever—God dwells. From heaven, He rules the heavens and the earth, sends punishments on the unrighteous, and calls sinners to Himself through His Son, Jesus Christ.

This sheds light on the other passages that speak of someone's going to heaven. Revelation 11 speaks of the two prophets of God who testify against the unrighteous servants of the beast and weigh out God's wrath on those who oppose them. However, at the end of a certain period of time, they are killed and their bodies lie in the streets for three-and-one-half days, at which time the Lord raises them from the dead. John writes, (v. 12) "Then they heard a loud voice from heaven saying to them, 'Come up here!' And they went up to heaven in a cloud, and their enemies watched them." This is not the story of a dead person who went to heaven. It is the story of two people who were killed *and then raised from the dead* who were then taken into heaven, much as Elijah was in 2 Kings 2:1. In other words, when this passage tells us that the two prophets went to heaven, it is not telling us what happens to people after they die.

The only other places that speak of people going to heaven are Matthew 11:23 and Luke 10:15. Since Luke 10:15 has the same words as Matthew 11:23 in a different context, we will look only at Matthew, where Jesus is dealing with opposition to His ministry. He points out that people were not willing to accept John the Baptist, who separated himself from the normal social rituals surrounding eating and drinking, but people were also not willing to accept Jesus, because He was involved in the normal social rituals of eating and drinking. (Matthew 11:20) "Then He began to denounce the cities where most of His mighty works had been done, because they did not repent." Matthew 11:23 is His denunciation of Capernaum: "And you, Capernaum, will you be exalted to heaven? You will be brought down to Hades. For if the mighty works done in you had been done in Sodom, it would have remained until this day." Several clues tell us that this passage is not about the fate of believers after they die. First, the passage refers to an entire city rather than an individual. Second, it does not mention dying. Third, the context makes clear that Jesus is speaking about the Day of Judgment, when He will return to judge the living and the dead. Matthew 11:24 reads, "But I tell you that it will be more tolerable on the day of judgment for the land of Sodom than for you."

Oddly enough, then, the Bible does not explicitly say that believers go to heaven when they die. Neither does it say that unbelievers go to hell when they die. That is not to say that you have to give up everything you ever believed—far from it. The ideas conveyed by the words "Grandpa is in heaven now" may well be in line with what the Bible says. However, exploring what the Bible says in more detail and depth may give us even more comfort than our everyday ideas give us. So, what *does* happen to us after we die?

3 The Brief Guided Tour

In the Apostles' Creed, we confess, "I believe in . . . Jesus Christ, . . . who . . . suffered under Pontius Pilate, was crucified, died and was buried. He descended into hell. The third day He rose again from the dead. . . . I believe in the Holy Spirit, . . . the resurrection of the body, and the life everlasting." These words, carefully crafted to convey the truths of the Scriptures, give us a pattern for the doctrines of heaven and hell. Because of our sin, we human beings die. Death, however, is not the end. Both believers and unbelievers continue on in the state of death until Jesus comes again, when He will raise both believers and unbelievers from the dead. Unbelievers He will send away to hell. Believers, on the other hand, He will take to heaven—that is, to the kingdom God prepared for them before the world was created, the New Jerusalem.

In speaking of heaven and hell, then, we should really distinguish among three time frames: the days of a person's life here on earth, the time between a person's death and the second coming of our Lord, and the time (or, rather, eternity) after Jesus' second coming. Because something important and decisive happens on the day when Jesus comes again, we should be careful not to skip over that day when we talk about heaven and hell. The state of human beings—dead and alive—before that day will be radically different than their state after that day.

Before Judgment Day, believers who have died will be with Christ. As we saw earlier in this lecture, our traditional words "in heaven" are used in the Bible to reflect the presence of God. We are therefore right to say that believers who have died are in heaven, so long as we understand that heaven is not simply a holding place for the dead or a location like any other. Heaven is where God dwells, and believers who have died rest from their labors in the presence of God. The important part here is not where (some place called heaven) but with whom (with Christ). Moreover, believers who have died and are with Christ in heaven are not yet what they will be. Their souls and spirits have separated from their bodies, and their souls and spirits have gone to the Lord in heaven, but they are still dead. They are safe from harm, and they can no longer sin, but neither are they physically alive. It is not until Jesus returns that they will then receive their bodies and enter the age to come.

Unbelievers who have died, on the other hand, are not with Christ. They went without Christ in life, and so they go without Christ in death. It is still true to say that their souls and spirits separate from their bodies, and it is still true to say that they are not yet what they will be. They, too, will be raised on the Last Day. Until then, however, their bodies return to the dust of this creation, and their souls and spirits are kept in a place called Sheol until the Day of Judgment. We will learn more about Sheol in the next session, but the upshot is that it is a place of darkness and weakness, and it is without God's gracious presence.

Sheol is not what we typically think of as hell, however. Both the Gospel of Matthew and the Revelation to St. John make clear that unbelievers will be sent away from God to a place of terrible, bodily torment after the resurrection of the dead. That is hell. Hell is terrible, because there "their worm does not die and the fire is not quenched" (Mark 9:48). Skin burns and blisters, but the nerves never lose their ability to feel the pain. Worms eat at the inside, but they never go so far as to finish a person off. Dante's claim that there are different levels of hell is fanciful imagination without any real basis in Scripture; in fact, the medieval picture of demons and devils tormenting unbelievers is probably also far from the truth, because the lake of fire is meant for the devil and his angels. They too will suffer in their own way for their disobedience against God.

Thankfully, our gracious God made a way out for us sinful human beings. Because His Son rose from the dead and is now glorified at His right hand, believers will also be glorified in the resurrection. We will receive back our bodies, but the bodies we receive back will be glorified. Moreover, we will no longer suffer any kind of hunger, pain, loss, disease, or sickness. Just as God walked with Adam and Eve in the beginning, so will it be in the end. Of that time, God declares, (Revelation 21:3) "Behold, the dwelling place of God is with man. He will dwell with them, and they will be His people, and God Himself will be with them as their God." Heaven will be a place of utter joy, where our bodies work the way they were meant to and where we have the intimate communion with God that He intended for us.

Conclusion

Naturally, we will get into details in the coming sessions. In the next session, we will look more closely at the so-called interim state, that is, the state of believers and unbelievers between death and the second coming of Jesus. The following two sessions will explore what the Old and New Testaments have to say about hell. We will look specifically at questions about God's justice and the important role of hell in giving comfort to persecuted Christians. Then we will turn our eyes to the doctrine of heaven, spending three sessions getting a glimpse of the eternal joys prepared for us at God's right hand. Finally, we will finish the Bible study with a session about living heavenward.

Concluding Activities

Speak a closing prayer, make any necessary announcements, and distribute study leaflet 2.

"Daddy, What Happens When We Die?"

Selected Passages

Preparing for the Session

Central Focus

The Bible has many ways of referring to death, all of which point to our true comfort as Christians: that those who die in the faith rest from their labors in this world and remain safe with Christ until He raises them from the dead to live with Him forever.

Objectives

That participants, led by the Holy Spirit working through God's Word, will

1. understand the distinction between the interim state and the resurrection;
2. explain what Jesus means by referring to death as "sleeping";
3. give a biblical explanation of the interim state of the righteous and the unrighteous; and
4. find comfort in the rest enjoyed by those who die in the faith.

Note for the small-group leaders: Lesson notes and other materials you will need begin on page 59.

For the Lecture Leader

Session Plan

Worship

Begin the session with the hymn printed in the study leaflet. Accompaniments are available in denominational hymnals, such as *Lutheran Service Book* or *Lutheran Worship* (refer to hymnal index). (Note: Concordia Publishing House has available *The Concordia Organist*, a 31-CD collection of pipe organ accompaniments for all the hymns and liturgical music in *Lutheran Service Book*. All the initial worship hymns in the LifeLight courses are included in this resource. It's especially helpful for mission congregations and small parishes. See the list of study resources on p. 7.) Follow with this prayer:

Prayer

Almighty God, grant Your unworthy servants Your grace, that in the hour of our death the adversary may not prevail against us, but that we may be found worthy of everlasting life; through Jesus Christ, our Lord. Amen. (*LSB Altar Book*, p. 453)

Lecture Presentation

Introduction

The coffin stands at the front of the room. People have come to pay their last respects. They look at the pictures set up near the coffin, laugh over good memories, and then take a few moments to view the body. After they file past the coffin, they offer their condolences to the family of the deceased. Suddenly, a little child in the line turns to his father and asks, "Daddy, what happens when we die?" Our basic, traditional answer is that the believer who dies goes to heaven, and the unbeliever goes to hell. Our slightly more sophisticated, traditional answer is that the soul and body of the individual separate at death. The body remains here on earth, and the soul of the deceased goes to heaven if he is a believer or to hell if he is an unbeliever. On the Last Day, soul and body are reunited in the resurrection; Christians go to heaven, and non-Christians go to hell.

As we saw in the first session, the Bible does not use the phrase "go to heaven" to describe what happens to believers after they die. In the remainder of this session, we will see what the Bible *does* say about the state of believers and unbelievers who die. Theologians refer to the state between death and the resurrection as "the interim state." As the word *interim* implies, this is an in-between state. The dead in Christ have not yet received the full glory that will be theirs in the resurrection, and dead unbelievers have not yet been consigned to their eternal punishment. Nevertheless, the dead in Christ rest from their labors in this world and remain safe with Christ until He raises them from the dead to enjoy life in the age to come.

1 What Happens When We Die

We know from experience that the body stops functioning when a person dies. In fact, we often equate death with the cessation of bodily function. One or more organs begin to fail for whatever reason, and after a time they can no longer sustain all the processes that keep the body going. When those processes stop, the person has died. However, if you have ever been present when another person has died, you may have felt that something more was going on. In fact, Lutheran pastor and ethicist Gilbert Meilaender has argued that the respect we show to the corpse of a dead person proves we believe death is not simply the end of a biological process. Something mysterious, even transcendent, occurs at death.

While the Scriptures do not give us a detailed account of dying, they do help us understand what that mysterious, even transcendent element of death is. In mundane terms, the soul and the spirit separate from the body. The Scriptures use both words: *soul* and *spirit*. Genesis describes the death of Rachel by saying that she named her newborn son Ben-oni "as her soul was departing (for she was dying)" (35:18). Likewise, in describing the death of a wealthy man in one of His parables, Jesus has God say, "Fool! This night your soul is required of you, and the things you have prepared, whose will they be?" (Luke 12:20). In yet another example, when the son of the widow of Zarephath became ill and died, Elijah "stretched himself upon the child three times and cried to the Lord, 'O Lord my God, let this child's life come into him again'" (1 Kings 17:21). The word here translated as "life" is the same word translated "soul" in Genesis 35:18. On the other hand, Matthew describes the death of Jesus by saying that He "yielded up His spirit" (27:50), and John writes similarly that Jesus "gave up His spirit" (19:30). (The two evangelists use slightly different verbs, but the meaning is the same.) Luke recounts how "Jesus, calling out with a loud voice, said, 'Father, into Your hands I commit My spirit!'" (23:46), and he further writes in the Book of Acts that Stephen called out, "Lord Jesus, receive my spirit" (7:59) as he was being stoned to death. Ecclesiastes encourages us to remember the Creator in the days of our youth, before "the dust returns to the earth as it was, and the spirit returns to God who gave it" (12:7)—that is, before we die. In other words, the Scriptures bear witness that we are more than simply biological beings, and that death is more than simply the end of a biological process. Life involves body, soul, and spirit, and "the body apart from the spirit is dead" (James 2:26). When we die, soul and spirit separate from the body.

However, that does not answer the child's question. If soul and spirit separate from the body when we die, where do they go? What happens to the soul and spirit of the believer after death, and what happens to the soul and spirit of the unbeliever after death? For the remainder of this session, we look at each of these questions in turn, before dispelling a few myths about those who have died.

2 Unbelievers after Death

If the Bible says little about the state of believers between death and the resurrection of the dead, then it says even less about the state of unbelievers during that time. The New Testament has one straightforward passage: 1 Peter 3:19, which explains that Christ "went and proclaimed to the spirits in prison" after His death (what the Apostles' Creed calls His descent into hell). These are the spirits who "formerly did not obey, when God's patience waited in the days of Noah, while the ark was being prepared" (1 Peter 3:20). A second passage also gives us hints of the state of unbelievers after death; although there is debate among interpreters whether this account is a parable or a realistic situation. Jesus tells the story of a rich man who died, and (Luke 16:23–24) "in Hades, being in torment, he lifted up his eyes and saw Abraham far off and Lazarus at his side. And he called out, 'Father Abraham, have mercy on me, and send Lazarus to dip the end of his finger in water and cool my tongue, for I am in anguish in this flame.'" If this account gives us a description of the state of believers and unbelievers after death, then we should expect that unbelievers are already suffering from unquenchable fire (a theme to which we return in the next session). Moreover, there is no escape; as Abraham says to the rich man in the parable, (Luke 16:26) "between us and you a great chasm has been fixed, in order that those who would pass from here to you may not be able, and none may cross from there to us." Other passages in the New Testament that describe the fate of unbelievers either definitively refer to them after the resurrection of the dead at the coming of our Lord Jesus Christ or are vague as to whether they refer to the state of dead unbelievers prior to the resurrection or after it.

The Old Testament, however, has a bit more to say about the state of unbelievers after death. Psalm 9:17 says, "The wicked shall return to Sheol, all the nations that forget God." Generally speaking, the Old Testament uses the word *Sheol* to describe where unbelievers go after they die. Proverbs 5:5, for example, says that an adulteress's "feet go down to death; her steps follow the path to Sheol." What is more, even believers who are experiencing sorrow and suffering often speak as if they will end up in Sheol. Psalm 88:3 gives voice to this sentiment. The psalmist cries out to God to hear him, saying, "for my soul is full of troubles, and my life draws near to Sheol." The patriarch Jacob likewise expressed his sorrow this way when he heard that his son Joseph had (supposedly) died. (Genesis 37:35) "All his sons and all his daughters rose up to comfort him, but he refused to be comforted and said, 'No, I shall go down to Sheol to my son, mourning.' Thus his father wept for him." Jacob seems to be saying, "Joseph met a terrible end, and because his life ended with sorrow and suffering, he will see Sheol, and I will too because of my sorrow and suffering."

For the sake of clarity, you should know that the Old Testament sometimes uses the word *Sheol* in a more neutral sense, as the resting place of all the dead, righteous and unrighteous alike. In fact, the word has been interpreted in different ways, even among Lutheran theologians. However, all Lutheran theologians agree that those who die without faith do not enter the presence of God, while those who do die in faith enjoy God's presence in between death and the resurrection. The details of how we interpret the word *Sheol* do not lead to differences in doctrine among Lutherans.

What is Sheol like? It is a place of weakness (Isaiah 14:9–11). It is a place of darkness (Psalm 49:13–20). God's wrath against idolatry reaches even into Sheol (Deuteronomy 32:22). People in Sheol do not praise God (Psalm 6:5). Despite our curiosity, the Scriptures do not give us much information about Sheol or about the state of unbelievers between death and the resurrection of the dead. This much, however, we do know. Those who by God's grace believe in God's promise of salvation through Jesus Christ enjoy a different state after death, because the Lord has redeemed us.

3 Believers after Death

Psalm 49 stands as a stark admonition to us human beings to remain humble before God. (vv. 13–15) "This is the path of those who have foolish confidence; yet after them people approve of their boasts. Like sheep they are appointed for Sheol; death shall be their shepherd, and the upright shall rule over them in the morning. Their form shall be consumed in Sheol, with no place to dwell. But God will ransom my soul from the power of Sheol, for He will receive me." The Old Testament is clear: if Sheol refers to the state of unbelievers after death, then believers have a different fate, because the Lord purchases us from Sheol. We can choose to walk in the ways of the adulteress, but "her house is the way to Sheol, going down to the chambers of death" (Proverbs 7:27). However, "the path of life leads upward for the prudent, that he may turn away from Sheol beneath" (Proverbs 15:24). Our gracious God does not want any of His creatures to go down to Sheol. He therefore instructs us with His Word, which shows us our Savior, Jesus, who by His blood redeemed us. Those who have faith in Him will not join unbelievers in Sheol. In the beautiful words of King David, (Psalm 86:13) "Great is Your steadfast love toward me; You have delivered my soul from the depths of Sheol."

The Scriptures use a variety of imagery to refer to the death of believers. The Old Testament says of the patriarchs that they were gathered to their people (Genesis 25:8; 49:33; Numbers 20:26; 31:2; Deuteronomy 32:50). The Books of Judges, Kings, and Chronicles speak of being gathered to one's fathers and being gathered to the grave (Judges 2:10; 2 Chronicles 34:28—parallel to 2 Kings 22:20). Psalm 73:24 even refers to dying as being received into glory: "You guide me with Your counsel, and afterward You will receive me to glory." What all these images have in common is an emphasis on community. Believers who die are not isolated from those who went before them in the faith, and they are not isolated from our gracious Father in heaven. On the contrary, believers who die have only been transferred from the Church Militant (the communion of God's people still struggling against the devil, the world, and our own sinful human nature) to the Church Triumphant (the communion of God's people who rest from their labors). Dead believers are still part of the Holy Christian Church that we confess in the Apostles' Creed.

Other passages in the Old Testament, and many in the New Testament, refer to death as sleep. Examples include Psalm 13:3, "Consider and answer me, O Lord my God; light up my eyes, lest I sleep the sleep of death"; Daniel 12:2, speaking of the resurrection of the dead, "many of those who sleep in the dust of the earth shall awake"; 1 Kings 1:21, where Bathsheba refers to David's impending death by saying, "when my lord the king sleeps with his fathers"; Matthew 9:24, where Jesus says of a girl who has died, "Go away, for the girl is not dead but sleeping"; and 1 Corinthians 15:6 and 1 Thessalonians 4:14, where Paul refers to the dead as those who "have fallen asleep." Sleep as an image for death is particularly comforting. It implies rest from the wearisome troubles of the day as well as a time when those sleeping will wake up refreshed. We do not normally fear sleep, and if death is akin to sleep, then we have no need to fear death either. In the words of the hymn "All Praise to Thee, My God, This Night" (*LSB* 883:3), "Teach me to live that I may dread the grave as little as my bed." When our Lord Jesus comes again, we will be awakened to meet Him face-to-face.

Other passages in the New Testament speak of death as departing in peace or departing to be with Christ. The peace of which Simeon sings in Luke 2:29 is the peace of a believer who has seen the promises of God fulfilled in his life. The Lord had promised Simeon he would see the Christ, and when Simeon held Jesus, he knew God had kept His promise. Simeon could depart this life in peace because God, who had kept the promise of the Messiah, would keep all of His promises. Paul, on the other hand, writes in Philippians 1:23, "My desire is to depart and be with Christ." His point is that he is not afraid to die for preaching Christ crucified, and in fact he would prefer to die rather than to continue suffering the hardships of his ministry, because after death he would be with Christ. Paul does not mean that Christ is not with us now, because Jesus promised, (Matthew 28:20) "I am with you always, to the end of the age." However, "now we see in a mirror dimly" (1 Corinthians 13:12). Christ is with us, but we experience Him through means rather than directly. After death, Christians are with Christ in a new way. As Jesus said to the thief on the cross, (Luke 23:43) "Truly, I say to you, today you will be with Me in Paradise." Because Jesus Christ gave His life on the cross for us and rose from the dead as "the firstfruits of those who have fallen asleep" (1 Corinthians 15:20), death no longer means separation from God but rather the enjoyment of God's presence in Christ.

Just as important, death means rest. The apostle John relates, (Revelation 14:13) "I heard a voice from heaven saying, 'Write this: Blessed are the dead who die in the Lord from now on.' 'Blessed indeed,' says the Spirit, 'that they may rest from their labors, for their deeds follow them!'" Christians who die no longer struggle against the devil, because they are beyond temptation. They no longer struggle against the world, because they have departed the world to be with Christ. They no longer struggle against their own sinful natures, because their sinful natures have met their ultimate demise, begun in the waters of Baptism and consummated in the death of the body. They no longer suffer, and they no longer worry, and they no longer sin. Their labors are done. (Hebrews 4:9–10) "So then, there remains a Sabbath rest for the people of God, for whoever has entered God's rest has also rested from his works as God did from His."

To be sure, death remains God's just judgment against our sin, for "the wages of sin is death" (Romans 6:23). Yet, Jesus took this judgment on Himself in our place, and He rose from the dead. (Romans 6:10) "The death He died He died to sin, once for all, but the life He lives He lives to God." Paul can therefore exult, (1 Corinthians 15:55–57) "'O death, where is your victory? O death, where is your sting?' The sting of death is sin, and the power of sin is the law. But thanks be to God, who gives us the victory through our Lord Jesus Christ." Christians need not fear death, because our Savior, Jesus, transformed it into the gateway to eternal life. Death is the final defeat of our own sinful natures, and when we die, our Savior, Jesus, receives us into His glory to rest from all our labors until He comes again to raise us to everlasting life. The intimate communion Christ shares with believers here continues on after death.

4 So Grandpa's Looking Down on Me?

Before we move on to the next session, we need to address a couple of myths about the dead. The first myth is that the dead become angels. They do not. Angels are beings created by God as spirits. They do not by nature have physical, fleshly bodies the way you and I do. An angel without a body is an angel, but a human being without a body is, well, dead. An angel is not simply a disembodied soul but a unique creature with its own mode of existence. People who die do not suddenly turn into a different sort of being; rather, people who die remain dead until the Lord raises them—and us all—from the dead on the Last Day. Unfortunately, some people support this myth by referring to Matthew

22:30, where Jesus says, "in the resurrection they [those who are raised to eternal life] neither marry nor are given in marriage, but are like angels in heaven." Two points are worth noting about this passage. First, Jesus is referring to the resurrection—that is, to the state of believers after Jesus returns to judge the living and the dead. He is not describing the state of people between death and the resurrection. Second, Jesus does not say that believers will be angels after the resurrection; instead, He says that they will be like angels in one respect—that they will not marry. Believers will be risen, glorified human beings, not angels.

The second myth we must address is that the dead look down on this world and have specific knowledge of our particular lives. I suspect you have heard people give voice to this opinion; you may even have expressed it yourself. While the sentiment can be comforting in some ways, it does not square with what the Scriptures say. In sleep, we become more or less oblivious to the world around us, and death is like sleep in that way. The dead are certainly safe with our Savior, Jesus, and they enjoy the presence of Christ (Philippians 1:23; Luke 16:19–31; Revelation 14:13). A few passages in Revelation (e.g., 6:10) portray the martyrs (those who died for the sake of the faith) calling out to God in the words of the Psalms, "O Sovereign Lord, holy and true, how long before You will judge and avenge our blood on those who dwell on the earth?" (E.g., Psalms 13:1–2; 35:17; 74:10). Nothing in the Bible, however, suggests that the dead are able to keep track of what is going on in our lives. While it may be comforting to feel as though they are sharing our joys (and sorrows) from heaven, we should draw our true comfort from the fact that they are experiencing the joys of God's glory, and that God Himself keeps watch over us.

Conclusion

We cannot talk about heaven and hell without also understanding what the Bible says about death. Thankfully, the Bible does not give us a clinical, theoretical explanation of death. Instead, God's Word comforts Christians in the face of this great enemy of ours by reminding us that Jesus Himself has experienced it and defeated it. Paul writes, (1 Thessalonians 4:13) "We do not want you to be uninformed, brothers, about those who are asleep, that you may not grieve as others do who have no hope." We confess that Jesus Christ died and rose from the dead, so we also confess that Jesus has defeated death for us. For Christians, death is therefore the final judgment on the sinful nature, which was sentenced to death in Baptism, and it is a departure from this world of struggle to the glories of Christ's presence in heaven. The psalmist writes, (116:15) "Precious in the sight of the LORD is the death of His saints." What amazing power our Lord wields, to take the judgment against our sin and turn it into the gateway to eternal communion with God. (Revelation 14:13) "'Blessed are the dead who die in the Lord from now on.' 'Blessed indeed,' says the Spirit, 'that they may rest from their labors'"

Concluding Activities

Speak a closing prayer, make any necessary announcements, and distribute study leaflet 3.

The Justice of God and the Fate of the Wicked, Part 1

Selected Passages

Preparing for the Session

Central Focus

On Judgment Day, God will condemn unbelievers to hell, but His judgment is just, because they have rejected His Son despite His attempts to convert them through His Word.

Objectives

That participants, led by the Holy Spirit working through God's Word, will

1. gain an understanding of what will happen on Judgment Day;
2. explain why God is just in condemning some people to hell;
3. describe the terrible torments of hell, based on New Testament passages; and
4. find comfort in the fact that hell was not created for humanity but for the devil and his angels.

Note for the small-group leaders: Lesson notes and other materials you will need begin on page 61.

For the Lecture Leader

Session Plan

Worship

Begin the session with the hymn printed in the study leaflet. Accompaniments are available in denominational hymnals, such as *Lutheran Service Book* or *Lutheran Worship* (refer to hymnal index). (Note: Concordia Publishing House has available *The Concordia Organist,* a 31-CD collection of pipe organ accompaniments for all the hymns and liturgical music in *Lutheran Service Book.* All the initial worship hymns in the LifeLight courses are included in this resource. It's especially helpful for mission congregations and small parishes. See the list of study resources on p. 7.) Follow with this prayer:

Prayer

We implore You, O Lord, in Your kindness to show us Your great mercy that we may be set free from our sins and rescued from the punishments that we rightfully deserve; through Jesus Christ, our Lord. Amen. (*LSB Altar Book,* p. 451)

Lecture Presentation

Introduction

Some of the most graphic, troubling descriptions of hell come from Jesus. It is Jesus who gives us the most comprehensive description of Judgment Day, and it is Jesus who will sit on the judgment throne. It is Jesus who speaks those devastating words to unbelievers: (Matthew 25:41) "Depart from Me, you cursed, into the eternal fire prepared for the devil and his angels." Judgment and eternal punishment are an undeniable part of Jesus' message, and we cannot sidestep them without discounting His message. In this session, we will explore these difficult words in depth in order to understand what happens on Judgment Day and why. We will also see what other New Testament writings say about Judgment Day and hell. Finally, we will reflect on God's grace and mercy in Christ.

1 Judgment Day (Matthew 25:31–46)

As we saw in the previous session, the time between a person's death and the second coming of Jesus is called the interim state. At Jesus' second coming, all who have died—both believers and unbelievers—will be raised from the dead. This is what we confess in the Apostles' Creed: "I believe in . . . the resurrection of the body." When Jesus raises the dead, He will also judge them all. The most comprehensive description of Judgment Day comes to us from Jesus and is recorded in Matthew 25:31–46, which you read this past week.

Several points are worth noting. First, when Jesus comes, all nations will be gathered before Him. This includes every man, woman, and child who is alive at the time, as well as every man, woman, and child who has ever lived. No human being will escape Judgment Day. In the Revelation, John expresses it this way: (20:12) "And I saw the dead, great and small, standing before the throne, and books were opened."

Second, our Lord Jesus really will judge. (Matthew 25:32) "He will separate people one from another as a shepherd separates the sheep from the goats." Some people claim that a loving God could not or would not consign anyone to hell. They argue that Jesus Christ died for the sins of every person, so no one will spend eternity in hell. However, the unambiguous testimony of the Scriptures is that God will separate the righteous from the unrighteous, believers from unbelievers, and that each group will experience a different fate in eternity. The Lord says as much in Daniel 12:2: "And many of those who sleep in the dust of the earth shall awake, some to everlasting life, and some to shame and everlasting contempt." Jesus' words in Matthew 25 leave no doubt about the fact, either. Our Father is gracious and merciful, so much so that He sent His own Son to take on our human flesh and die for our sins, but "God is not mocked, for whatever one sows, that will he also reap" (Galatians 6:7). The forgiveness that Christ won on the cross does not imply the abolition of hell.

Third, Jesus judges on the basis of deeds. This may be difficult for Christians to swallow, since we rightly confess, (Ephesians 2:8–9) "by grace you have been saved through faith. And this is not your own doing; it is the gift of God, not a result of works, so that no one may boast." At the same time, the clear testimony of the Scriptures is that Jesus will judge the living and the dead based on their deeds. Here in Matthew 25, Jesus sends away those who gave Him no food when He was hungry, gave Him no drink when He was thirsty, did not greet Him when He was a stranger, and so on. Likewise, the apostle John relates, (Revelation 20:12) "the dead were judged by what was written in the books, according to what they had done."

In the end, however, these statements need not worry us. The fact is, although we are not saved by works, faith nevertheless works. (James 2:17) "Faith by itself, if it does not have works, is dead." (Luke 6:45) "The good person out of the good treasure of his heart produces good, and the evil person out of his evil treasure produces evil, for out of the abundance of the heart his mouth speaks." Whether the works listed in Matthew 25 refer to general deeds of charity or whether, as is more likely, they refer to acts of hospitality shown to Christians who suffer persecution because they publicly confess the Good News about Jesus, the point is still the same. People without faith do not respond to basic human needs in the same way believers do. People without faith lack the works of faith, just as people with faith do not lack the works of faith. When our Lord Jesus says He will judge people based on their works, He understands those works as fruits or public testimonies of faith.

Fourth, and perhaps most important, the eternal fire to which unbelievers are sent was not prepared for them. Jesus draws a careful distinction in the reading: the kingdom that believers inherit was prepared for them from the foundation of the world, but the eternal fire to which unbelievers are sent was prepared "for the devil and his angels" (Matthew 25:41). God did not decide before creation or just after the fall that certain people would go to hell. (He did elect certain people to go to heaven, but that is a discussion for another Bible study.) Hell was not created for people, because our gracious God does not want any people to be in hell. (Ezekiel 33:11) "As I live, declares the Lord God, I have no pleasure in the death of the wicked, but that the wicked turn from his way and live." He takes so little pleasure in the death of the wicked that He gave His own Son into death on a cross as "the propitiation for our sins, and not for ours only but also for the sins of the whole world" (1 John 2:2). So that all people could hear the Good News about Jesus, God called apostles and He still calls pastors and missionaries to preach. He gives parents and grandparents the wonderful opportunity (and the grave responsibility) to tell their children and grandchildren about Jesus. He gives each Christian opportunities to share the Good News with family members, co-workers, and neighbors. (Romans 10:13–15) "For 'everyone who calls on the name of the Lord will be saved.' How then will they call on Him in whom they have not believed? And how are they to believe in Him of whom they have never heard? And how are they to hear without someone preaching? And how are they to preach unless they are sent?" Our Lord sends people to preach because hell was not created for human beings.

2 Hell

Unfortunately, although it was not created for human beings, there will still be human beings in hell. The tragic fact is that some people reject the Good News about Jesus Christ, and others never hear it. Paul wrote, (2 Thessalonians 1:8–10) "Those who do not know God and . . . those who do not obey the gospel of our Lord Jesus . . . will suffer the punishment of eternal destruction, away from the presence of the Lord and from the glory of His might, when He comes on that day to be glorified in His saints." Or, in the words of Revelation 20:15, "If anyone's name was not found written in the book of life, he was thrown into the lake of fire." Despite Christ's sacrifice on the cross, and despite the Spirit's work to proclaim the Good News through the preaching of God's Word, some human beings will remain without faith and will end up in hell.

As we have seen, Revelation describes hell as a lake of fire. The phrase is first used in Revelation 19:20, where John writes that the great beast who opposed God was "thrown alive into the lake of fire that burns with sulfur" along with his false prophet. In the following chapter (20:13–15), John recounts how "the sea gave up the dead that were in it, Death and Hades gave up the dead that were in them. . . . Then Death and Hades were thrown into the lake of fire. This is the second death, the lake of fire. And if anyone's name was not found written in the book of life, he was thrown into the lake of fire." God says to John in Revelation 21:8, "But as for the cowardly, the faithless, the detestable, as for murderers, the sexually immoral, sorcerers, idolaters, and all liars, their portion will be in the lake that burns with fire and sulfur, which is the second death." Finally, an angel says to John in Revelation 14:9–10, "If anyone worships the beast and its image and receives a mark on his forehead or on his hand, he also will drink the wine of God's wrath, poured full strength into the cup of His anger, and he will be tormented with fire and sulfur in the presence of the holy angels and in the presence of the Lamb."

Older translations of the Bible use the word *brimstone* instead of *sulfur*. Most of us imagine hell as a dark, fiery place in shades of red, but sulfur actually burns blue in the presence of oxygen (not that God is limited by the laws of this creation). As it burns, it produces sulfur dioxide, a gas with a suffocating odor. Revelation says unbelievers are thrown into a lake that burns with fire and sulfur. There is no escape. There is no island or shore where they might find respite, and some part of their bodies will always be in the lake. We must be careful, however, not to read this passage too literally. For one thing, it comes from Revelation, which is full of images not meant to be taken literally. For another, Revelation 20:14 says that Death and Hades were thrown into the lake of fire. While this certainly signifies God's ultimate victory, death and hades are treated here with a literary device called personification. They are treated as persons who can be thrown into a lake.

On the other hand, other New Testament passages also speak of hell as place of fiery torment. In Matthew 25:41, Jesus tells unbelievers, "Depart from Me, you cursed, into the eternal fire prepared for the devil and his angels." Elsewhere in Matthew, Jesus refers to it as "the hell of fire" (Matthew 5:22; 18:9) and "the fiery furnace" (Matthew 13:42, 50). In Mark 9:43, He calls it "the unquenchable fire." But perhaps Jesus' most disturbing description of hell comes in Mark 9:47–48, where He is emphasizing how serious sin is. He says, "And if your eye causes you to sin, tear it out. It is better for you to enter the kingdom of God with one eye than with two eyes to be thrown into hell, 'where their worm does not die and the fire is not quenched.'" Scholars debate the exact meaning of the final clause (which is a quotation from Isaiah 66:24). Some say the fire never ends and the worm never dies, because new material is always added to hell. On this interpretation, Jesus is not saying that the individual suffers forever, but rather that there is always someone new being added. However, by quoting Isaiah 66:24, Jesus makes clear that He is referring to the ultimate victory of God over all who oppose Him. That is Judgment Day. Nowhere else do the Scriptures suggest that unbelievers are gradually added to hell after the final judgment. Rather, as Jesus indicates in Matthew 25:46, the punishment of each wicked person will be eternal, just as the life of each believer will be eternal.

The word used for *hell* in the New Testament, *Gehenna*, refers to the Valley of Hinnom outside of Jerusalem. The valley had been used in Old Testament times as a place to sacrifice children, by fire, to the false god Molech. In Jesus' day, it was used by the inhabitants of Jerusalem as a place to burn garbage and the bodies of dead criminals. It likely smoldered day and night with a suffocating, smoky fire. Maggots and other vermin would feed on the rotting garbage, only adding to the stench. If you have been severely burned in a fire, you may want to tune out for a moment. Imagine for a moment that your body has been infested with those worms. They eat away at your flesh. Normally, you would eventually weaken to a point that you would no longer feel the pain. But imagine now that your body somehow always has enough tissue for the worm not only to continue feeding on you, day after day, but also for the pain to continue, day after day, without any hope of respite. Again, imagine being trapped in a fire from which there is no escape, a fire that never goes out. Every movement only causes the fire to flare up around you and covers your skin with new cinders. The heat burns and sears your flesh, but somehow your nerves stay intact so that you feel the excruciating pain minute after minute, day after day, without any hope of relief. That is hell.

Other words of Jesus reinforce the tremendous suffering of people in hell. When we imagine hell as a dark place, we are probably reflecting the passages in which Jesus refers to hell as "the outer darkness" (Matthew 8:12; 22:13; 25:30). In the first two of these passages, an individual is thrown out of a meal or celebration into the outer darkness. In the final passage, the individual is thrown out of the king's court. All three passages therefore imply that the outer darkness is a place far away from the light of God's presence and the joyful celebration of God's saints in the age to come. People in heaven "will need no light of lamp or sun, for the Lord God will be their light" (Revelation 22:5), but people in hell will have no light because God is not present. As we saw a moment ago, unbelievers "will suffer the punishment of eternal destruction, away from the presence of the Lord and from the glory of His might" (2 Thessalonians 1:9). If we wished to push the image a bit further, we could say that people in the darkness of hell do not even have the ability to find comfort or support from one another. Each suffers alone in darkness, apart from God and apart from the light of human company. Medieval depictions of hell show devils and demons tormenting the people who are in hell, but hell is as much a punishment for the devils and demons as for the people who rejected God. If the demonic horde has the satisfaction of tormenting human beings, they will nevertheless suffer terribly as well.

It is easy to understand why Jesus says several times, "in that place there will be weeping and gnashing of teeth" (Matthew 8:12; 13:42; 13:50; 22:13; 24:51; 25:30; Luke 13:28). One final element only intensifies the suffering. In several of these passages, Jesus tells the Pharisees that they will be cast out of God's kingdom for their unbelief, while many apparently unrighteous people will enter the kingdom of God through faith in Christ. When they see this, they will weep and gnash their teeth. The pain will be terrible for those who are in hell—first, the physical suffering from the eternal fire and the worm that does not die, second, the awful separation from God (and perhaps even from human company), and finally, the knowledge that people despised in this life are enjoying paradise. With no end in sight, with no release possible, they will only be able to weep and gnash their teeth in anger at God, despite the justice of His judgment. Even in hell, they will remain unrepentant.

3 Hell and the Justice of God

Human reason shies away from—even revolts at—the thought of hell. The agony and its duration seem out of proportion to the offenses. Many people object on the grounds that a loving God would never condemn anyone to such torment. While such thoughts are certainly rational, we must remember that our human reason is infected by sin just as much as our words and deeds. The truth about God is beyond anything our human reason can figure out on its own. Only when God reveals the truth about Himself can we know it, and the truth He has revealed is this: (Exodus 20:5; Deuteronomy 5:9) "I the Lord your God am a jealous God, visiting the iniquity of the fathers on the children to the third and the fourth generation of those who hate Me." God takes sin seriously. When Adam and Eve ate the fruit of the tree of the knowledge of good and evil, God sentenced them and all their offspring to death, just as He had said He would. He sentenced them to death because no creature can have life apart from the Creator who gives life. By seeking sustenance and wisdom in the fruit rather than in God's Word, Adam and Eve separated themselves from God, who gives life. They hid from Him in the garden. Running away from Him means running away from life. Ultimately, it means running toward hell.

We must remember that each one of us deserves to go to hell. God does not rescue us Christians from the wrath to come because we are somehow better than other people. He does not rescue us from the fiery furnace because we are in any way different from other people. He rescues us from hell only by His grace, as a free gift, because His Son, Jesus Christ, died on the cross to pay the penalty no human being could pay. This salvation is available to all people, and the Spirit puts that Good News on the lips of Christians—pastors and laypeople alike—in order to rescue as many people as possible from the fires of hell, despite the fact that each of us deserves those fires. (Romans 6:23) "The wages of sin is death, but the free gift of God is eternal life in Christ Jesus our Lord."

God sentences some people to hell, then, because He is a just God. In sending people to hell, He is giving them no more than they deserve. In fact, in sending them to hell, He is doing no more than cementing the choice they made in life to not worship the one true God. They will spend eternity without the true, life-giving God whom they would not worship in life, and they will spend eternity suffering God's wrath for rejecting His Son, Jesus Christ, who took that wrath on Himself.

That anyone goes to heaven rather than hell is entirely a gift.

Concluding Activities

Speak a closing prayer, make any necessary announcements, and distribute study leaflet 4.

The Justice of God and the Fate of the Wicked, Part 2

Selected Passages

Preparing for the Session

Central Focus

Hell is not simply God's way of punishing unbelievers for ignoring Him; it is also His way of protecting His people from persecution and mistreatment by unbelievers.

Objectives

That participants, led by the Holy Spirit working through God's Word, will

1. explain why God's judgment is just;
2. describe hell as it is portrayed in the Old Testament; and
3. find comfort in the vindication and protection that hell provides for believers.

Note for the small-group leaders: Lesson notes and other materials you will need begin on page 63.

For the Lecture Leader

Session Plan

Worship

Begin the session with the hymn printed in the study leaflet. Accompaniments are available in denominational hymnals, such as *Lutheran Service Book* or *Lutheran Worship* (refer to hymnal index). (Note: Concordia Publishing House has available *The Concordia Organist*, a 31-CD collection of pipe organ accompaniments for all the hymns and liturgical music in *Lutheran Service Book*. All the initial worship hymns in the LifeLight courses are included in this resource. It's especially helpful for mission congregations and small parishes. See the list of study resources on p. 7.) Follow with this prayer:

Prayer

Almighty God, unto whom all hearts are open, all desires known, and from whom no secrets are hidden, cleanse the thoughts of our hearts by the inspiration of Your Holy Spirit that we may perfectly love You and worthily magnify Your holy name; through Jesus Christ, our Lord. Amen. (*LSB Altar Book*, p. 451)

Lecture Presentation

Introduction

If you go online to look up "hell in the Old Testament," you will turn up any number of Web sites claiming that the doctrine of hell is not in the Old Testament. They rightly point out that the word *hell* appears in the King James Version of the Bible as a translation of the Hebrew *Sheol*, and then they rightly point out that Sheol is not a place of punishment for unbelievers after the resurrection. As we saw in Session 2, Sheol is where the souls of unbelievers are kept until the resurrection of the dead. Depending on how literally we read Jesus' parable in Luke 12, Sheol may or may not include a component of suffering.

However, the concept of a place where unbelievers experience God's wrath after the resurrection is present in the Old Testament. In this session, we will see that several Old Testament prophecies envisioned a time when unbelievers would be separated from God's presence and from other believers. These prophecies are meant for the comfort of God's people, who suffer injustice at the hands of unbelievers in this age. In this session, we will examine some of these prophecies, revisit the justice of God's judgment, and finally learn to find comfort in the doctrine of hell.

1 "The Days Are Coming"

The people of Israel lived in difficult times. They lived among nations who worshiped false gods. As if that were not enough, they had kings who led them in worshiping idols, priests who neglected the temple and the Word of God, prophets whose prophesied for money, rulers who oppressed the poor, and judges who took bribes. In 931 BC, the twelve tribes of Israel, who had been united as one kingdom under David's son Solomon, split into two kingdoms: Israel (or Samaria) in the north and Judah (with its capital in Jerusalem) in the south. In 722 BC, the Northern Kingdom was destroyed by Assyrian armies as God's judgment against their unceasing idolatry. Unfortunately, the kings in the south did not learn their lesson, even though they were the descendants of King David. In 587 BC, the Babylonian army marched into Jerusalem, burned down the temple, set up an occupation government, and took most of the educated and skilled people into exile. Again, this was God's judgment against the people of Judah for their idolatry. However, God did not destroy them, because He had promised that a Savior would come from among them, from the descendants of David.

The writings of the prophets address this terrible state of affairs. On the one hand, the prophets boldly and explicitly identified the people's sins, often at great peril to themselves. On the other hand, the prophets also spoke of a time when injustice and idolatry would come to an end. Through Jeremiah, for instance, the Lord said, (23:5) "Behold, the days are coming, declares the LORD, when I will raise up for David a righteous Branch, and He shall reign as king and deal wisely, and shall execute justice and righteousness in the land." These words were spoken both to comfort the believers who suffered at the hands of unbelievers as well as to give hope to people who might repent when the Lord executed His judgment through the armies of Babylon. As we will see, these promises of a righteous ruler were fulfilled in the life, death, and resurrection of our Savior, Jesus.

Before we dive in, you should know that many Christians understand these passages differently than we do. They understand "Judah" and "Israel" to refer to the genetic descendants of Abraham. However, John the Baptist hints that God is not limited to the genetic descendants of Abraham in keeping His promises; when he chastises the Sanhedrin for coming to his baptisms, he preaches, (Matthew 3:9) "Do not presume to say to yourselves, 'We have Abraham as our father,' for I tell you, God is able from these stones to raise up children for Abraham." As it turns out, (Galatians 3:7) "It is those of faith who are the sons of Abraham." In Christ Jesus, Gentiles have been grafted into the people of God; meanwhile, anyone who does not believe in Jesus Christ has been cut out of the family tree of Abraham. I, therefore, take all the passages we will look at to refer to God's gracious action in Christ Jesus for all people.

While Daniel wrote later than Isaiah, his vision of Judgment Day provides a good introduction to the fate of the wicked. He writes, (12:2) "Many of those who sleep in the dust of the earth shall awake, some to everlasting life, and some to shame and everlasting contempt." The word *many* has the connotation of a large number; it does not mean "many" as opposed to "all." Rather, the word *many* refers to the multitude—the whole, huge, uncountable mass of humanity. Everyone who has died will be raised from the dead, and those whose names are not written in "the book" (Daniel 12:1) will be raised to shame and everlasting contempt. Whatever else hell is, it is eternal, and it involves both shame and contempt. Contempt here probably refers to God's contempt—that is, God does not make His face shine on them, is not gracious to them, and does not lift up His countenance upon them. Instead, He casts them away from Himself forever.

Isaiah offers an even more vivid description:

> (1:24–31) Therefore the Lord declares, the LORD of hosts, the Mighty One of Israel: "Ah, I will get relief from My enemies and avenge Myself on My foes. I will turn My hand against you and will smelt away your dross as with lye and remove all your alloy. And I will restore your judges as at the first, and your counselors as at the beginning. Afterward you shall be called the city of righteousness, the faithful city."
>
> Zion shall be redeemed by justice, and those in her who repent, by righteousness. But rebels and sinners shall be broken together, and those who forsake the LORD shall be consumed. For they shall be ashamed of the oaks that you desired; and you shall blush for the gardens that you have chosen. For you shall be like an oak whose leaf withers, and like a garden without water. And the strong shall become tinder, and his work a spark, and both of them shall burn together, with none to quench them.

Here the Lord God is declaring that the city of Jerusalem, which had succumbed to idol worship, oppression, drunkenness, injustice, and other great shame and vice, will one day have judges who refuse to take bribes. It will have leaders—counselors—who guide the people in the right direction. It will eventually be known for its righteousness, and the people will eventually be noted for their faithfulness to the Lord. On the other hand, all those who rebel against God's Word and break His Law will wither and be burned like tinder, like small, dry twigs.

Clearly, those who rebel against God have not yet burned. Nor can we even say that the people who bear God's name (that is, us Christians) are universally known for our righteousness and faithfulness. Christians still fall, sometimes badly. Injustice still occurs, even within the church. For this reason, we can see this passage from Isaiah to be looking forward to the end of time. He is speaking of the final judgment, when the righteous will be glorified before the world and the wicked will finally meet God's judgment. While Isaiah does not explicitly refer to an eternal fire, he does say that the wicked will burn with a fire that no one can quench. The rebels and sinners will be powerless to escape the Lord's wrath against their sinfulness.

Micah 5 draws a picture of the restoration of God's people. Through Micah, God says, (5:8–9) "The remnant of Jacob shall be among the nations, in the midst of many peoples, like a lion among the beasts of the forest, like a young lion among the flocks of sheep, which, when it goes through, treads down and tears in pieces, and there is none to deliver. Your hand shall be lifted up over your adversaries, and all your enemies shall be cut off." Jacob, the grandson of Abraham, wrestled with God and had his name changed to Israel. The "remnant of Jacob," therefore, refers to the children of Jacob who remained faithful to God—that is, those with faith in Christ. The time is coming, God says, when believers will no longer fear unbelievers. Unbelievers will no longer be a factor in our lives. They will not be able to persecute us any longer. God goes on to say that He will remove every idol. He will get rid of their chariots, because the people had put their trust in military might rather than the God who had brought them out of Egypt. He will get rid of sorcery and fortune-telling and all of the statues the people had worshiped. Then, He says, (Micah 5:15) "In anger and wrath I will execute vengeance on the nations that did not obey." Anyone who continues to violate God's Word will fall under God's wrath.

Micah's words here are echoed in Revelation 21:25–27: The holy city's "gates will never be shut by day—and there will be no night there. They will bring into it the glory and the honor of the nations. But nothing unclean will ever enter it, nor anyone who does what is detestable or false, but only those who are written in the Lamb's book of life." In the holy city, the new Jerusalem—that is, in our eternal life with God—we will not worry about attackers who would force us to close the gates in order to protect the city. There will not be anyone left to attack the people of God. People who never repented of their sins will not enter the city. As John writes a few verses earlier, (v. 8) "As for the cowardly, the faithless, the detestable, as for murderers, the sexually immoral, sorcerers, idolaters, and all liars, their portion will be in the lake that burns with fire and sulfur, which is the second death."

God's desire to protect His people from their persecutors is even more explicit in Joel 3:17–21. The passage begins with a God-centered description of the age to come: "So you shall know that I am the Lord your God, who dwells in Zion, My holy mountain. And Jerusalem shall be holy, and strangers shall never again pass through it." In other words, the people will no longer worship false gods but will instead recognize the true God as their God. Moreover, no strangers (that is, no one who brings false gods) will enter the holy city of Jerusalem. After a verse that describes the fertility of the newly renewed land, the passage continues in what modern ears hear as a more negative tone: (v. 19) "Egypt shall become a desolation and Edom a desolate wilderness, for the violence done to the people of Judah, because they have shed innocent blood in their land." Egypt was, of course, the nation that had enslaved the Israelites. Edom was the nation of the descendants of Esau, the brother of Jacob. Although the Edomites were cousins to the Israelites, the Edomites would not let the Israelites pass through their land on the journey from Egypt to the Promised Land. Later, when the people of Jerusalem fled the invading Babylonian army, the Edomite army not only stood by but actually attacked the people of Judah. Egypt and Edom are mentioned here, then, as the enemies of God's people. They have shed the innocent blood of God's people, and God will not let the deed go unanswered. The passage closes, (v. 21) "I will avenge their blood, blood I have not avenged, for the Lord dwells in Zion." This passage does not have unambiguous heaven-and-hell language. However, the way in which it describes Jerusalem as holy and promises that no strangers shall enter make a strong link to the Revelation of St. John, as does the idea that the people will finally acknowledge that the Lord God is the true God. No city will be perfectly holy until our Lord returns to judge the living and the dead, so it is not difficult to read this passage as a description of what will happen in the age to come. God's vengeance against those who persecuted His people will be a very real part of the age to come. In other words, hell is real.

2 Justice

The talk of vengeance probably makes most of us uncomfortable, particularly in light of Jesus' words, (Matthew 5:39) "If anyone slaps you on the right cheek, turn to him the other also." In fact, from early on in Christian history, people have tried to rescue the Christian faith from the vengeance passages of the Old Testament. One pastor named Marcion (pronounced MAR-see-uhn), living around AD 100, was so put off by the Old Testament vengeance passages that he taught that the Old Testament god was different from the New Testament God, whom Jesus called Father. He revised the canon—the list of the books in the Bible—by removing all the books of the Old Testament. While few people have gone as far as Marcion did, the idea that the Old Testament portrays a vengeful god while the New Testament portrays a loving God has persisted right up to our own day. This idea is even reflected in an old but mistaken saying among some that the Old Testament shows us the Law while the New Testament shows us the Gospel.

The previous session, in which we considered New Testament passages about hell, should convince us that nothing could be further from the truth. In fact, Jesus Himself tells the Pharisees, (Matthew 23:34–35) "Therefore I send you prophets and wise men and scribes, some of whom you will kill and crucify, and some you will flog in your synagogues and persecute from town to town, so that on you may come all the righteous blood shed on earth, from the blood of righteous Abel to the blood of Zechariah the son of Barachiah, whom you murdered between the sanctuary and the altar." There are enough passages of this kind that Marcion not only removed the Old Testament from the Bible, but he also edited the New Testament significantly to remove them. However, if you find yourself editing the Scriptures because they don't fit your idea of what you think they should say, then your idea of what the Scriptures say is wrong. The Old Testament proclaims God's vengeance against sin, and so does the New Testament. Likewise, the New Testament proclaims God's mercy to sinners, and as we will see in coming sessions, so does the Old Testament.

However, we also need to be careful not to misunderstand what the Scriptures say about God's vengeance. In this life, we Christians turn the other cheek in order to bear witness to the divine patience that God has toward us—patience so great that the Lord has not yet entirely destroyed our human race, despite our sin. Rather than taking vengeance into our own hands, we wait for the Lord, who has declared, (Deuteronomy 32:35) "Vengeance is Mine, and recompense." It is not our job to implement the Old Testament laws in order to straighten out the moral climate of our nation. It is not our job to punish, persecute, or otherwise penalize unbelievers. Rather, we proclaim the Law of God (what He demands from us and what the consequences of failure are), and we proclaim the Gospel of Jesus Christ ([2 Corinthians 5:19] "that is, in Christ God was reconciling the world to Himself, not counting their trespasses against them"). Within the church, we call people to repentance without seeking revenge. Outside the church, we do the same thing. We love our enemies and pray for those who hate us (Luke 6:27–28).

Yet the Lord reserves vengeance for Himself. While we pray for the conversion of our enemies, we also take comfort in the fact that our gracious Father will not leave us to the devices of our tormenters forever. The day will come when they will finally have exhausted the mercy of God, and He will show them the same lack of mercy that they showed to His people. We tend to measure justice in terms of duration—a punishment that lasts forever appears unjust compared to persecution that lasted only a short time (relatively speaking). However, God's justice is based on the dispositions of those who oppose Him. If they are unmerciful, then He will deal with them unmercifully. If they have rejected His forgiveness in Christ, then He will withhold it from them. If they have tried to win His love by their good deeds (or lack of bad deeds), then He will judge them according to their deeds, which are evil, because they break the first three commandments.

We can thus identify three ways in which God's judgment—that is, hell—serves justice. First, (Romans 5:12) "sin came into the world through one man, and death through sin, and so death spread to all men because all sinned." From the time we are born, our hearts and minds are set against the one true God. We try worshiping Him with our works rather than seeking His mercy, thus breaking the First Commandment. We develop all kinds of fanciful doctrines and attach God's name to them rather than calling on the God who has revealed Himself in the Scriptures, thus breaking the Second Commandment. We rebel against His Word rather than taking His Word to heart, thus breaking the Third Commandment. In other words, the default human condition is to deserve hell. God is not unjust for condemning anyone to hell. He would not be unjust to condemn you to hell. You deserve it, and so does everyone else.

Second, God treats the unmerciful unmercifully in the judgment. Those who opposed God's people, persecuted them, made fun of them, and the like will receive from God the exact kind of treatment that they doled out to God's people. God's judgment is not arbitrary. In a sense, one could speak of poetic justice. Those who rejected Jesus Christ get to face God's wrath on their own rather than finding safety from it under the cross. Those who wanted a life without Christians will get a life without people who show mercy. Most of all, we can see that those who in this life did not humble themselves before God in Christ will continue to shake their fists at God in Christ throughout all eternity. Even in their suffering, they will not seek God's mercy.

Third, justice demands that victims receive redress. Our own justice system acknowledges this principle and tries to enact it, however imperfectly. A teenager who is caught bashing in mailboxes receives punishment, and part of the punishment is to make the victims whole. The teenager will have to pay for new mailboxes. To take an even more disturbing example, a husband who physically abuses his wife can be punished by the court system, and part of the punishment can be redress for the wife in the form of a restraining order. The restraining order is not simply a mean-spirited attempt to punish the man; it is a means by which the court protects the woman from further abuse by her husband. If the court system fined the man but then let him return to hurting his wife, we would say it had failed to do justice. By analogy, if God brought believers into eternal life with Him but let unbelievers continue to persecute us, then He would not really have protected us. Justice demands that He protect His people from those who wrongly persecute them. Hell serves precisely that purpose.

Conclusion

God is never acting unjustly when He sends someone to hell. He has nevertheless taken all the steps necessary to ensure that no one need spend eternity in hell. (John 3:16) "For God so loved the world, that He gave His only Son, that whoever believes in Him should not perish but have eternal life." In other words, His mercy overrides justice in the first sense. Moreover, He not only sent His Son, Jesus Christ, but He also sent prophets and apostles to proclaim the Good News that heaven is ours through Jesus Christ, and He continues to send pastors, church workers, and ordinary Christians to share that Good News with one another and with the world. He shows His mercy to people like you and me, unmerciful though we are, in order to call us into His kingdom. Along the way, His Holy Spirit softens our hearts so that we begin to show the same kind of mercy toward others that God shows toward us. (1 John 4:19) "We love because He first loved us." In this way, God's mercy overrides justice in the second sense. Finally, God calls you and me to pray for our enemies, and He provides for the Word to be proclaimed even to those who persecute His people. In other words, God's mercy even overrides justice in the third sense by seeking to make Christians out of critics and followers out of foes.

Concluding Activities

Speak a closing prayer, make any necessary announcements, and distribute study leaflet 5.

The Mercy of God and the Fate of the Redeemed

Selected Passages

Preparing for the Session

Central Focus

On Judgment Day, Jesus will raise both believers and unbelievers from the dead. He will invite believers to inherit the kingdom of God, and He will give them new, glorious, spiritual bodies like His.

Objectives

That participants, led by the Holy Spirit working through God's Word, will

1. distinguish between the resurrection of the dead and the life everlasting;
2. explain what happens to believers on the Last Day; and
3. look forward to the second coming of Jesus with joy.

Note for the small-group leaders: Lesson notes and other materials you will need begin on page 65.

For the Lecture Leader

Session Plan

Worship

Begin the session with the hymn printed in the study leaflet. Accompaniments are available in denominational hymnals, such as *Lutheran Service Book* or *Lutheran Worship* (refer to hymnal index). (Note: Concordia Publishing House has available *The Concordia Organist*. All the initial worship hymns in the LifeLight courses are included in this resource. It's especially helpful for mission congregations and small parishes. See the list of study resources on p. 7.) Follow with this prayer:

Prayer

Almighty, everlasting God, You gave Your only Son to be a High Priest of good things to come. Grant unto us, Your unworthy servants, to have our share in the company of the blessed for all eternity; through Jesus Christ, our Lord. Amen (*LSB Altar Book*, p. 453).

Lecture Presentation

Introduction

If you have read many end-times books, you know that their dominant theme is how fearful those times will be. Our modern representations echo what Jesus says about the last times: (Luke 21:25–26) "There will be signs in sun and moon and stars, and on the earth distress of nations in perplexity because of the roaring of the sea and the waves, people fainting with fear and with foreboding of what is coming on the world." The problem is, most of the modern representations aim at scaring you into believing. They depict the end times graphically so that you become a believer and avoid the tribulations by being raptured away before they occur. Aside from the fact that believers will not be raptured away before the final judgment, modern depictions suffer from one other defect: they do not have the same aim as the Scriptures. When Jesus describes the terrible events of the end times, He further says to believers, (Luke 21:28) "Now when these things begin to take place, straighten up and raise your heads, because your redemption is drawing near." In this session, we will learn what joy awaits Christians on the day when Jesus comes to judge the living and the dead.

1 Waiting and Watching

We have already learned that those who die in Christ will be with Christ. They await the second coming in the safety of God's presence, free from the trials and tribulations of this world. They are in heaven, meaning that their souls and spirits are in God's care. They are not yet enjoying the full-blown resurrection life of which both the Scriptures and the creeds speak. They are sleeping until our Savior comes to raise them from the dead.

Those of us who are still alive are likewise waiting, and hopefully we are following Jesus' advice to be watching, (1 Thessalonians 5:2) "for you yourselves are fully aware that the day of the Lord will come like a thief in the night." We are quite conscious of the trials and tribulations of this world. Knees that give out, ongoing cancer treatments, the bitter sadness of losing a child—all these trials remind us that we live in a world beset by sin and its effects. Terrorist attacks, wars, geopolitical instability—these likewise remind us that the divisions among the nations have not yet been healed. Like the saints in heaven who await the coming of our Lord, we also wait and watch.

Thankfully, that day will come, because our Lord has promised it will come. (2 Peter 3:9) "The Lord is not slow to fulfill His promise as some count slowness, but is patient toward you, not wishing that any should perish, but that all should reach repentance." God's justice demands that He punish those who have persisted in rejecting Him and His Son, and God's mercy moves Him to give eternal life to those whom He has chosen. For believers, that day will be a "great and awesome day" (Joel 2:31), because it will mean the end of our waiting and the complete, full-bodied enjoyment of everlasting life in the presence of God—Father, Son, and Holy Spirit.

2 "The Resurrection of the Body, and the Life Everlasting"

In the Apostles' Creed, we confess, "I believe in . . . the resurrection of the body, and the life everlasting." These two phrases refer to two distinct events. "The resurrection of the body" refers to the general resurrection of all the dead, both believers and unbelievers, on the Last Day. God said to Daniel, (12:2) "Many of those who sleep in the dust of the earth shall awake, some to everlasting life, and some to shame and everlasting contempt." All the dead will be raised up with physical bodies to stand before the judgment throne of Christ. Revelation speaks in much the same way: (20:13) "The sea gave up the dead who were in it, Death and Hades gave up the dead who were in them, and they were judged, each one of them, according to what they had done." Jesus said, (John 5:28–29) "Do not marvel at this, for an hour is coming when all who are in the tombs will hear His voice and come out, those who have done good to the resurrection of life, and those who have done evil to the resurrection of judgment."

This does not mean, however, that both believers and unbelievers will enter eternal life. "Life everlasting" is the gift Jesus purchased for all people but which is taken in hand only by those who have faith in Jesus. Unbelievers will continue in their bodily existence forever, but nowhere do the Scriptures call their existence eternal life. Instead, the Scriptures say, (2 Thessalonians 1:9) "They will suffer the punishment of eternal destruction, away from the presence of the Lord and from the glory of His might." Eternal life comes only to those who have faith in Christ. In Jesus' words, (John 11:25) "I am the resurrection and the life. Whoever believes in Me, though he die, yet shall he live."

3 The Fate of the Righteous in the Resurrection

So what will happen to believers at the resurrection? Paul gives us a clear picture of the events of that day.

> (1 Thessalonians 4:14–17) Since we believe that Jesus died and rose again, even so, through Jesus, God will bring with Him those who have fallen asleep. For this we declare to you by a word from the Lord, that we who are alive, who are left until the coming of the Lord, will not precede those who have fallen asleep. For the Lord Himself will descend from heaven with a cry of command, with the voice of an archangel, and with the sound of the trumpet of God. And the dead in Christ will rise first. Then we who are alive, who are left, will be caught up together with them in the clouds to meet the Lord in the air, and so we will always be with the Lord.

Some Christians in Paul's day believed that people who died before Jesus' second coming would not be raised at the resurrection. Paul responds that they will, in fact, rise from the dead. We Christians need not mourn for our loved ones who died in Christ as if they are now lost forever. When Jesus comes back, both Christians who have died and those who are alive will see the One for whom they have been waiting.

To understand various descriptions of that day, we must first understand that no single passage lays out an agenda for the entire Day of Judgment. Each passage has a particular goal, and it presents enough information to achieve its goal. Some passages, such as 1 Thessalonians 4, are intended to comfort Christians who have lost loved ones to death. Other passages, such as the parable of the sheep and the goats in Matthew 25:31–46, speak of the final judgment of all people without explicitly mentioning the resurrection. Yet other passages, such as Daniel 12:1–3 and Revelation 20:11–15, mention both the general resurrection and the judgment without focusing on what happens to believers at the resurrection. The fact that 1 Thessalonians 4:13–17 does not mention unbelievers should not lead us to conclude that it is referring to some separate event, such as a pre-tribulation rapture of believers. This passage simply speaks words of comfort by affirming that those who die in the faith will greet Jesus and enter life everlasting on the Last Day.

First Corinthians 15:20–26 has a similar focus. Paul is once again responding to a claim that the dead in Christ will not rise from the dead (v. 12: "that there is no resurrection of the dead"). He first points out that Jesus Himself rose from the dead, (v. 20) "the firstfruits of those who have fallen asleep." Since Christ was raised from the dead, (vv. 22–24) "so also in Christ shall all be made alive. But each in his own order: Christ the firstfruits, then at His coming those who belong to Christ. Then comes the end, when He delivers the kingdom to God the Father after destroying every rule and every authority and power." These verses mention nothing about unbelievers or the judgment, but their language and the events they narrate clearly refer to the second coming of Christ. By pointing out that the second coming of Jesus will bring the resurrection of those who have died in Christ, these words bring comfort to those whose believing friends and family have died. On that day, both those who have died in Christ and those who remain alive will come into the presence of our loving Savior, Jesus, and He will bring us into the eternal kingdom of His Father.

A bit later in the chapter, Paul responds to another question: (15:35) "How are the dead raised? With what kind of body do they come?" He responds, (vv. 51–52) "Behold! I tell you a mystery. We shall not all sleep, but we shall all be changed, in a moment, in the twinkling of an eye, at the last trumpet. For the trumpet will sound, and the dead will be raised imperishable, and we shall be changed." Again, Paul does not mention the general resurrection, although he is talking about the Last Day. Rather, he focuses on what will happen to believers when we are raised from the dead. Unlike unbelievers, who will be raised to shame and everlasting contempt, believers will be changed. Both those who have died in the faith and those who are still alive at the coming of our Lord Jesus will put on imperishable, glorious resurrection bodies. (v. 53) "For this perishable body must put on the imperishable, and this mortal body must put on immortality." On that day, Jesus will replace the perishable bodies of living Christians with imperishable, spiritual bodies. Likewise, those who had died in the faith will be raised from the dead, their spirits and souls united with their new, imperishable, spiritual bodies. (vv. 42–44) "What is sown is perishable; what is raised is imperishable. It is sown in dishonor; it is raised in glory. It is sown in weakness; it is raised in power. It is sown a natural body; it is raised a spiritual body." Do not let the phrase "spiritual body" mislead you. When we modern Americans hear "spiritual," we think of something insubstantial, incorporeal, or ethereal, as if we lose our substantial, bodily existence and flit about like so many angels or spirits. That is not what Paul means. Rather, the phrase "spiritual body" stands in direct contrast to "natural body." The Greek word for "natural" appears in three other places in the New Testament: 1 Corinthians 2:14; James 3:15; and Jude 19. In all three passages, the word describes a person who is embedded in this sinful creation and fully opposed to God. It has the same meaning in 1 Corinthians 15—the natural body is embedded in this sinful order. Paul says of it, (Romans 7:23) "I see in my members another law waging war against the law of my mind and making me captive to the law of sin that dwells in my members." The spiritual body, on the other hand, will be free of this sinful creation and its effects. When Jesus raises all the dead from their graves, we believers will put off our old, natural bodies that are bound to this sinful world, and we will put on the new, spiritual bodies that belong in the new heavens and the new earth. (1 Corinthians 15:54–57) "When the perishable puts on the imperishable, and the mortal puts on immortality, then shall come to pass the saying that is written: 'Death is swallowed up in victory.' 'O death, where is your victory? O death, where is your sting?' The sting of death is sin, and the power of sin is the law. But thanks be to God, who gives us the victory through our Lord Jesus Christ."

To summarize, while both believers and unbelievers will be raised from the dead in the resurrection of the body, they will be raised in different ways. The Scriptures say nothing about the body with which unbelievers will be raised, but we can infer that it will be the natural body—a body that is still subject to weakness, pain, and sinful rebellion against God. On the other hand, believers will be raised from the dead with new, spiritual bodies, and believers who are alive will also receive new bodies. Our new bodies will be actual, fleshly, substantial bodies, just as Jesus Christ had an actual, substantial, fleshly body after His resurrection, because Jesus "will transform our lowly body to be like His glorious body, by the power that enables Him even to subject all things to Himself" (Philippians 3:21). As spiritual bodies, our bodies will no longer be afflicted by sin and its effects. They will never betray our desire to serve God and please Him. They will never experience weakness, pain, or decay. They will be perfect and glorious, just as the resurrection body of Jesus is perfect and glorious. (Matthew 13:43) "The righteous will shine like the sun in the kingdom of their Father."

4 The Red Carpet to Eternity

We looked at the parable of the sheep and the goats in Session 3 to see what happens to unbelievers on the Last Day. In today's session, we look at it again to see what happens to believers, and why. You may want to open your Bible to Matthew 25:31–40 to look back at what you read earlier.

The words that Jesus speaks to believers are full of wonderful meaning—not just because they roll out the red carpet to heaven for us, but also because they have the entire story of salvation encapsulated in them. Jesus begins with the wonderful word "come." Whenever Jesus says, "Come," He is inviting people into His presence to enjoy His blessings. In Matthew 4:19, He says to Peter and Andrew, "Come after Me, and I will make you fishers of men." (The ESV says, "Follow Me," but the Greek is literally "come after Me.") Matthew 11:28 has words we know well: "Come to Me, all who labor and are heavy laden, and I will give you rest." In Matthew 22:4, Jesus likens the kingdom of heaven to a king who invites people to the wedding feast of his son, saying, "See, I have prepared my dinner, my oxen and my fat calves have been slaughtered, and everything is ready. Come to the wedding feast." Finally, the apostle John recounts how the risen Lord appeared to His disciples while they were fishing. After they realized it was Him, they came to shore and saw a fire with fish and bread. Then Jesus said to them, "Come and have breakfast" (John 21:12). On the Last Day, when Jesus says to believers, "Come," He will be inviting us to enjoy His blessings in His presence forever.

The next phrase in Matthew 25 describes the believers to whom Jesus is talking. He will call us (v. 34) to "Come, you who are blessed by My Father." When the Scriptures say that God does the blessing, they imply that God is conveying benefits or showing favor to the one who is blessed. Jesus therefore bases His invitation to us to join Him for eternity on God's divine action toward us. We are not "you who have done enough good works to warrant salvation" or "you who have never struck out" or "you who have remained faithful." We are simply people blessed by the Father. While works will be evidence of our faith, Jesus does not roll out the red carpet to heaven for us because of our works. One could say that the red carpet is rolled out from God toward us so that we can enter His presence. It is not rolled out from us toward Him to indicate how important we are. We are recipients of God's blessing.

The main verb in the sentence in verse 34 reinforces that fact: "Come, you who are blessed by My Father, *inherit.*" By and large, a person does nothing to get an inheritance. It typically comes to a person upon the death of his or her parents. Trying to claim your inheritance before your parents die is sort of like wishing they were already dead—the way the younger son acted in the parable of the prodigal son (Luke 15:11–32). Trying to make yourself an heir to an estate involves deception (such as marrying a rich person on his or her deathbed or claiming blood relation when there is none). In the end, all you can typically do is establish that you should receive a share of the estate by virtue of your relationship to the deceased. When it comes to the eternal inheritance that belongs to us in Christ, the same is true. We cannot schmooze our way into the will or demand part of the estate on the basis of our behavior. We inherit only because we are children of God through faith in Jesus. We receive without any work on our own part what Jesus worked so hard to earn—eternal life.

The next phrase in verse 34 gives great evidence of the mercy of God. Jesus tells believers, "Inherit the kingdom prepared for you from the foundation of the world." God knew when He created us that we would fall into sin. However, He also knew when He created us that He wanted us to live with Him forever. Therefore, even from the time He created us, knowing we would sin, He prepared a kingdom for us to inherit eternally. He knew when He created us what it would cost Him to bring us into that kingdom: that He would send His Son, the Second Person of the Trinity, to be incarnate into our human flesh, to carry our sins on Himself, and to give His life on the cross. Nevertheless, because He loves us, He prepared a kingdom for us, and He created us although we would fall into sin, and He sent his Son to die for our sins. The lake of fire that is called hell was prepared for the devil and his angels, but the kingdom of God was prepared for sinful human beings who are in Christ.

Conclusion

The remainder of Matthew 25, which talks about the fate of the righteous at the final judgment, requires a bit of explanation. The reference to the good works of the righteous is not meant to imply that our good works earn us salvation. If that were the case, the kingdom of God would hardly be something to be inherited. Instead, it would be something to be received as wages or a reward. We are justified in God's sight solely through faith in Jesus Christ, but faith is never without good works. Those good works become the evidence of faith for the world around us, even at the judgment. In fact, in Revelation, a voice from heaven proclaims, (14:13) "Blessed are the dead who die in the Lord from now on," and the Spirit responds, "Blessed indeed, . . . that they may rest from their labors, for their deeds follow them!" With respect to earning salvation, the good works of the righteous are no better than filthy rags, but our gracious Father praises the righteous for our good works through Jesus Christ. As the righteousness of Christ covers each one of us like a robe, so the good works of the righteous clothe the Church. (Revelation 19:7–8) "'Let us rejoice and exult and give Him the glory, for the marriage of the Lamb has come, and His Bride has made herself ready; it was granted her to clothe herself with fine linen, bright and pure'—for the fine linen is the righteous deeds of the saints."

Concluding Activities

Speak a closing prayer, make any necessary announcements, and distribute study leaflet 6.

"Behold, the Dwelling Place of God Is with Man"

Selected Passages

Preparing for the Session

Central Focus

When we talk about eternal life, we tend to talk about going to heaven. The Scriptures, however, reveal a far richer picture of everlasting life. Our gracious Father will create new, perfect heavens and earth for believers, and He will live in that new creation with us forever.

Objectives

That participants, led by the Holy Spirit working through God's Word, will

1. understand the biblical concept of the new heavens and the new earth;
2. rejoice in the knowledge that God will dwell with His people; and
3. find courage and encouragement in the glory to come.

Note for the small-group leaders: Lesson notes and other materials you will need begin on page 67.

For the Lecture Leader

Session Plan

Worship

Begin the session with the hymn printed in the study leaflet. Accompaniments are available in denominational hymnals, such as *Lutheran Service Book* or *Lutheran Worship* (refer to hymnal index). (Note: Concordia Publishing House has available *The Concordia Organist,* a 31-CD collection of pipe organ accompaniments for all the hymns and liturgical music in *Lutheran Service Book.* All the initial worship hymns in the LifeLight courses are included in this resource. It's especially helpful for mission congregations and small parishes. See the list of study resources on p. 7.) Follow with this prayer:

Prayer

Lord God, our shepherd, You gather the lambs of Your flock into the arms of Your mercy and bring them home. Comfort us with the certain hope of the resurrection to everlasting life and a joyful reunion with those we love who have died in the faith; through Jesus Christ, Your Son, our Lord, who lives and reigns with You and the Holy Spirit, one God, now and forever. Amen. (*LSB Altar Book*, p. 397)

Lecture Presentation

Introduction

In the Gospel of Matthew, Jesus speaks of His final judgment, when He will call believers into the Father's kingdom. Paul comforts believers by teaching that those who died in the faith will receive new, glorified bodies on the Last Day. The prophets foresee a time when believers will no longer suffer persecution or fall into sin. These are wonderful sermons, but in many ways they pale in comparison to the Revelation of St. John in terms of describing the beauty and glory of everlasting life. In this session, we turn to John's description of what comes after the judgment. We also look at several Old Testament descriptions of the age to come. We will see that the word *heaven* hardly does justice to the glory of life in the age to come. Perhaps the voice that John heard from heaven says it best: (Revelation 21:3) "Behold, the dwelling place of God is with man. He will dwell with them, and they will be His people, and God Himself will be with them as their God." After the resurrection, believers will not be in heaven. Heaven will be with us.

1 New Heavens and a New Earth

If you think back to Session 1, you may remember that the word *heaven* has two meanings in the Bible. It can refer to the dwelling place of God. It can also refer to the part of creation above the sea and earth—the sky and outer space. Because heaven in the second sense is above us, we often say that heaven in the first sense is above us as well. The Bible talks about fire coming down from heaven, and it says that Jesus ascended—

that is, went up—into heaven. We must understand, however, that these directional words do not mean that heaven is in a particular location. You cannot punch in coordinates for heaven on your GPS. Heaven in the first sense is simply the presence of God, whom "heaven and the highest heaven cannot contain" (1 Kings 8:27). Heaven is about the person of God; it is not a particular place. In fact, the Bible does not typically speak of life after the resurrection as life in heaven. Various passages speak of our reward in heaven (Matthew 5:12; Luke 6:23), treasure in heaven (Matthew 19:21; Mark 10:21; Luke 18:22), citizenship in heaven (Philippians 3:20), and an inheritance kept in heaven (1 Peter 1:4). Because heaven is not a location, but is the presence of God, these passages mean that God is keeping our reward, treasure, and inheritance safe until Jesus brings us into His presence.

This is important because we live in a creation that consists of both heavens and the earth. (Genesis 1:1) "In the beginning, God created the heavens and the earth."God created them good, but our sin has corrupted them. Paul writes, (Romans 8:19–21) "For the creation waits with eager longing for the revealing of the sons of God. For the creation was subjected to futility, not willingly, but because of Him who subjected it, in hope that the creation itself will be set free from its bondage to corruption and obtain the freedom of the glory of the children of God." Because this creation has been corrupted by our sin, God will one day destroy it. According to Peter, (2 Peter 3:7) "By the same word [that created the world] the heavens and earth that now exist are stored up for fire, being kept until the day of judgment and destruction of the ungodly." He then explains, (v. 10) "The day of the Lord will come like a thief, and then the heavens will pass away with a roar, and the heavenly bodies will be burned up and dissolved, and the earth and the works that are done on it will be exposed." The entire creation will be destroyed. This doctrine is affirmed in the Old Testament as well: (Psalm 102:25–26) "Of old You laid the foundation of the earth, and the heavens are the work of Your hands. They will perish, but You will remain; they will all wear out like a garment. You will change them like a robe, and they will pass away."

We must keep two points in mind. First, when the Scriptures speak of heaven (or the heavens) and the earth passing away, they are not speaking of heaven in the sense of God's dwelling place but rather of that part of creation that is above the sea and the land. Second—and very important—even though heaven and earth will pass away, that does not mean we will suddenly be taken into the presence of God to live in the uncreated heaven where He dwells. The destruction of the heavens and the earth is not God's final act. Peter confesses, (2 Peter 3:13) "According to His promise we are waiting for new heavens and a new earth in which righteousness dwells." Everything we see around us now will pass away, but God will indulge in a second act of creation to give us new heavens and a new earth in which to live. As the apostle John wrote in Revelation 21:1, "I saw a new heaven and a new earth, for the first heaven and the first earth had passed away, and the sea was no more." Likewise, God said through Isaiah, (65:17) "Behold, I create new heavens and a new earth, and the former things shall not be remembered or come into mind."

God gave the apostle John a glorious vision of the new heaven and the new earth in Revelation 21. We have all been rightly taught that sin cannot enter the presence of our Holy God. God and sin cannot coexist. God Himself will come to us to live among us in the new heavens and the new earth, which means that they will have no sinful human beings. Those who hold on to their sin through impenitence will never enter the new heavens and the new earth, but will instead be thrown into the lake of fire. On the other hand, those who, through faith in Christ, repent of their sin and receive forgiveness have already been cleansed of their sin. When we are clothed with our new, glorious, spiritual bodies, the sinfulness of the natural body will be destroyed with this creation. We will finally be all saint and no sinner, and we will be able to live face-to-face with our gracious Father in the new heavens and the new earth. He will come to us, and we will live with Him forever.

2 Death Shall Be No More

In many ways, the Scriptures tell us very little about the nitty-gritty of life after the resurrection. We know that the Holy City Jerusalem will not have a temple, because we will have direct access to the triune God. We will no longer need to hear His Word through intermediaries such as pastors, teachers, and parents, because we will be living face-to-face with the Almighty God and the Lamb, His Son, Jesus Christ. Neither will the new creation have sun or moon or stars, because the old order of things will have passed away. God Himself and the Lamb will provide the light we need, and they will provide it all the time, so that there will never be any night. We who are living in the new heavens and the new earth will have no enemies to worry about, so the gates of the city "will never be shut by day" (Revelation 21:25). The city will be safe not because of its insurmountable walls, but because Jesus Christ will have won the final victory over our every enemy. He will have turned the tables, so that our enemies will be powerless to attack us. We will be safe.

Everything associated with sin in the old heaven and earth will be gone. Death is nothing less than God's curse against sinful human beings, but in the new heaven and the new earth, "death shall be no more" (Revelation 21:4). Illness and disease and pain and mourning and crying will likewise be things of the past. God even tells us through Isaiah, (65:25) "The wolf and the lamb shall graze together; the lion shall eat straw like the ox, and dust shall be the serpent's food. They shall not hurt or destroy in all My holy mountain." The age-old fear that animals have for humans, which God instilled in them after the flood (Genesis 9:2), will disappear, and the animals will be so changed that they will not present any danger to the citizens of the new heavens and the new earth. As Isaiah wrote elsewhere:

> (11:6–9) The wolf shall dwell with the lamb, and the leopard shall lie down with the young goat, and the calf and the lion and the fattened calf together; and a little child shall lead them. The cow and the bear shall graze; their young shall lie down together; and the lion shall eat straw like the ox. The nursing child shall play over the hole of the cobra, and the weaned child shall put his hand on the adder's den. They shall not hurt or destroy in all My holy mountain; for the earth shall be full of the knowledge of the Lord as the waters cover the sea.

This vision of everlasting life has many elements, but they all finally come back to the words John heard from heaven: (Revelation 21:3) "Behold, the dwelling place of God is with man. He will dwell with them, and they will be His people, and God Himself will be with them as their God." God is the one who vanquishes death, first through the resurrection of His Son, Jesus Christ, from the dead, and then by casting death into the lake of fire. God is the one who changes the animals so that you can trust your child to wander through woods that are crawling with snakes and lions. God is the one who defeats those who would attack His people. God is the one who forgives our sins and recreates us in the waters of Baptism so that we, through faith in Christ, can enter the Holy City. Finally, what makes the new heavens and the new earth to be "heaven" in any sense is that God Himself will dwell with us. We, who have for so long held onto tokens of God's grace, such as the body and blood of our Savior in the Sacrament of the Altar or the water of Baptism or the words of Absolution, will now have God Himself sitting before us on His throne with the Lamb who was slain for us. We, whose devotion to Christ was clouded by sleepiness, fatigue, boredom, worries, and whatever else distracts us from worship, will now have nothing to distract us from the glory of Christ. (1 Corinthians 13:12) "Now we see in a mirror dimly, but then face to face." We, whose bodies ached under the stress and strains of this sinful creation, will (Isaiah 35:6) "leap like a deer, and the tongue of the mute [will] sing for joy." Finally, we, who here mark our days by months and seasons and years because our lives will come to an end, will never worry about the joy coming to an end, because we will live with God forever. Death will be no more.

3 Will My Dog Be in Heaven?

We naturally have all kinds of questions about what the new heavens and the new earth will be like. Will my beloved dog be in heaven? Will I recognize my spouse? In the remainder of this session, we will look at a few of these questions and see what, if anything, the Bible has to say about them. The answers may not always suit us, but we must base our understanding of eternal life on the Scriptures rather than our feelings here on earth.

So what about your special dog? The short answer is simply that the Bible does not say. The kind of attachment we have toward our dogs, cats, and other pets was not generally shared by people in Jesus' day. In fact, in Jesus' day, Jews considered dogs unclean, and when the Scriptures mention dogs, it is nearly always in a negative light. However, as we saw earlier in this session, two passages from Isaiah talk about animals in heaven, including cattle and wolves. If we take those two passages literally, then the new heavens and the new earth will include animals, and they will live among us. What kind of attachments we will have to them is not clear. In the end, we can only say that God will give us everything we need to be happy and that we will be happy with whatever God has given us. Will you see your favorite dog or cat in heaven? We do not know, but if you do not, you will nevertheless enjoy communion with the God who gave you your pet in this age.

A more delicate question is whether we will recognize departed loved ones in the age to come. Again, the Bible does not give a straightforward answer. On the other hand, because relating to those dear to us is such an important part of life, we have no reason to believe that it will not also bring us great joy in eternity. There is a tension here that bedevils Christians from time to time: that of devotion to our gracious God and attachment to earthly creatures. In the Middle Ages, monks tried to resolve the tension by giving up earthly attachments in order to devote themselves to the worship of God. In our own day and age, many well-meaning Christians try to resolve the tension by quitting "a job" in order to undertake "a ministry," as if a common job excludes serving God. The other way to resolve the tension is to place so much attachment on human relationships that they keep us from confessing the Christian faith. The proper way to navigate this tension is to enjoy and rejoice in the human relationships we have, while understanding that they, like house, home, land, animals, money, and goods, are gifts from our heavenly Father. When it comes to everlasting life, our gracious Father may not ask us to resolve this tension by spending eternity worshiping Him to the exclusion of every other human activity. Instead, we may be able to enjoy human relationships in heaven as one more gift from our gracious God, and if so, then we will enjoy them without any friction or fighting *and* without any temptation to let those relationships become our gods. In short, we do not know exactly what our human relationships will be like in heaven, but we do know that they will be good through God's grace.

The same answer applies to spouses. Jesus makes it clear that we will not be married in heaven. Responding to some Sadducees who set up a rather far-fetched scenario to prove that there is no resurrection, Jesus said, (Luke 20:34–36) "The sons of this age marry and are given in marriage, but those who are considered worthy to attain to that age and to the resurrection from the dead neither marry nor are given in marriage, for they cannot die anymore, because they are equal to angels and are sons of God, being sons of the resurrection" (see also Matthew 22:30 and Mark 12:25). What Jesus says applies to the estate of marriage, which God instituted for this creation as part of His plan for humanity to "fill the earth and subdue it" (Genesis 1:28). In heaven, we will apparently live under a different mandate, so marriage and its procreative function will be unnecessary. However, if the Lord grants it, we will not only recognize but will also have great joy in being reunited with believing spouses in eternity. The union will not be marriage (nor could it be, since some Christians have survived more than one Christian spouse!), but it will have all the joy that God in His grace gives. Because life in God's presence will bring us perfect, eternal joys, we will have what we need to be happy, and we will be completely happy with whatever God gives us.

Finally, there is the difficult question of whether we will see the suffering of people who are in hell. While the answer is unsettling, the Scriptures suggest we will. At the end of Isaiah, God describes the new heavens and the new earth: (66:22–24) "For as the new heavens and the new earth that I make shall remain before Me, says the Lord, so shall your offspring and your name remain. From new moon to new moon, and from Sabbath to Sabbath, all flesh shall come to worship before Me, declares the Lord. And they shall go out and look on the dead bodies of the men who have rebelled against Me. For their worm shall not die, their fire shall not be quenched, and they shall be an abhorrence to all flesh." The passage is difficult for many reasons, but its claim that the saints in heaven will see the bodies of the rebels echoes other passages in Scripture. John writes in Revelation:

> (14:9–12) And another angel, a third, followed them, saying with a loud voice, "If anyone worships the beast and its image and receives a mark on his forehead or on his hand, he also will drink the wine of God's wrath, poured full strength into the cup of His anger, and he will be tormented with fire and sulfur in the presence of the holy angels and in the presence of the Lamb. And the smoke of their torment goes up forever and ever, and they have no rest, day or night, these worshipers of the beast and its image, and whoever receives the mark of its name." Here is a call for the endurance of the saints, those who keep the commandments of God and their faith in Jesus.

The passage is clearly talking about what we call hell—the eternal torment of unbelievers in the lake of fire and sulfur. Their torment takes place in the presence of the Lamb and the angels, which presumably means that God's people in the Holy City Jerusalem will also see it. The thought is likely a bit disturbing, but seeing the torment of God's enemies (and ours) will be a reminder of God's justice and a reminder of His mercy, which protects us from our enemies into all eternity.

Conclusion

Naturally, the questions about life in heaven could go on and on. Likewise, our speculations about daily activities, human relationships, religious observances, and the like could go on until Jesus returns. In the end, however, what matters is that our gracious God has given His Son, Jesus Christ, into death to rescue us from the wrath to come, and He has raised Him from the dead to give us everlasting life, and He will one day redeem us from this fallen world and all the attacks of the devil. On that day, we will inherit the new heavens and the new earth, and He will live with us as our God so that we can see Him face-to-face. In that day, we will pray with the Psalmist, (16:11) "You make known to me the path of life; in Your presence there is fullness of joy; at Your right hand are pleasures forevermore."

In the next two sessions, we will focus more specifically on the joys we will experience in heaven. In Session 7, we will explore how our ideas about heaven flow from our earthly desires, and then we will take a look at what it will mean for us to be sinless in the age to come. In Session 8, we will focus on the peace that Christians will enjoy in heaven—not just peace with God, but peace with one another.

Concluding Activities

Speak a closing prayer, make any necessary announcements, and distribute study leaflet 7.

"And They Will Be His People"

Selected Passages

Preparing for the Session

Central Focus

Our idea of heaven often reflects what we most love in this life. Thankfully, what heaven is like will not be decided by our desires, but by God in His grace and goodness. In heaven, we will have everything we want, and we will want only what God has given us.

Objectives

That participants, led by the Holy Spirit working through God's Word, will

1. describe how our earthly desires often color our ideas about heaven;
2. understand the relationship between the new creation and God's Law;
3. overcome worries about boredom in heaven; and
4. look forward to a time when our desires are in line with God's gifts.

Note for the small-group leaders: Lesson notes and other materials you will need begin on page 69.

For the Lecture Leader

Session Plan

Worship

Begin the session with the hymn printed in the study leaflet. Accompaniments are available in denominational hymnals, such as *Lutheran Service Book* or *Lutheran Worship* (refer to hymnal index). (Note: Concordia Publishing House has available *The Concordia Organist*, a 31-CD collection of pipe organ accompaniments for all the hymns and liturgical music in *Lutheran Service Book*. All the initial worship hymns in the LifeLight courses are included in this resource. It's especially helpful for mission congregations and small parishes. See the list of study resources on p. 7.) Follow with this prayer:

Prayer

Almighty and everlasting God, You knit together Your faithful people of all times and places into one holy communion, the mystical body of Your Son, Jesus Christ. Grant us so to follow Your blessed saints in all virtuous and godly living that, together with them, we may come to the unspeakable joys You have prepared for those who love You; through Jesus Christ, our Lord, who lives and reigns with You and the Holy Spirit, one God, now and forever. Amen. (*LSB Altar Book*, pp. 984–985)

Lecture Presentation

Introduction

Have you ever talked with a preteen about heaven? Many preteens envision heaven as either a perpetual worship service (read: really boring) or a 24/7 video-game extravaganza. Where do they get their ideas? It comes from hearing us talk about heaven. Sometimes we describe heaven as an eternal divine service—a prospect that sounds frightful to many preteens (and adults!). At other times, we depict heaven as if it will be all fun and no misery. Your typical preteen's idea of fun these days is playing video games and eating junk food, so preteens respond to this depiction enthusiastically. Both ways of thinking are mistakes. The first keeps us from looking forward to heaven, and the second gives us a twisted, sinful idea of heaven. Both mistakes stem from measuring heaven in terms of our earthly desires. In this session, we will look at how our earthly desires color our ideas about heaven, and then we will take a closer look at what our desires will be like in heaven.

1 Ideas of Heaven and Earthly Desires

Preteens are not the only people who let their ideas of fun in this life color their ideas of life in the age to come. Adults do too. Avid fishermen say something like, "In heaven I'll be able to fish all the time." People make jokes about deceased loved ones who are "in heaven playing cards" (notice the mixing up of the interim state and everlasting life in that statement, by the way). I have even heard people suggest that heaven will be wonderful because you will be able to eat whatever you want without worrying about your weight.

Perhaps the most glaring example of this mistake is the Muslim depiction of heaven. The Qur'an says that men who die in the cause of Allah will have a wonderful life in heaven. Each man will have seventy-two beautiful women at his disposal, each one of whom is a virgin and remains a virgin eternally (despite his having sexual intercourse with them). Sexual intercourse will last longer and be more pleasurable (for the man) than in this life. Moreover, young boys will serve the man and his virgins an exquisite feast. Martin Luther said of this idea of heaven, Muhammad "sets man's highest and final good (eternal blessedness) in fleshly desire" (*Luthers Werke: Kritische Gesamtausgabe*, vol. 53 [Weimar: Hermann Böhlau, 1920], 322; selection translated by Adam Francisco). The Muslim idea of heaven flows out of a male's earthly perspective on what would be most pleasurable. It simply takes earthly desires and projects them into the age to come. (More to the point, it takes the earthly desires of certain males and projects them into the age to come without any respect for the needs, desires, or comfort of women and children.)

Christians will have little trouble explaining the various mistakes with this version of heaven. For the moment, we are going to focus on one particular mistake: thinking that what I want in this life is what I will want in the life to come. In simple form, the line of thinking goes like this: (1) We will have eternal joy in heaven. (2) Right now, I enjoy such-and-such. (3) Therefore, in heaven, I will get to do such-and-such all the time. If I like fishing, then in heaven I will be able to fish as long as I like. If I like playing video games, then in heaven I can play video games all day.

The first statement, that we will have eternal joy in heaven, is true. The Scriptures state that God will give us eternal joys at His right hand (Psalm 16:11). Everything in this world that keeps us from enjoying God and His gifts will be destroyed. Fighting will cease, as will illness and death. It is true that we will have eternal, uninterrupted joy and pleasure in the life to come. The problem comes in the conclusion, which says, "since I enjoy such-and-such here, I will enjoy it in heaven." That is false. What we enjoy in this life is not necessarily what we will enjoy in the age to come. Why? Because our desires in this life are corrupted by sin, and in the age to come we will be without sin. Therefore, we may or may not enjoy in heaven what we enjoy here, even though we will enjoy whatever we do in the age to come.

The example of the Muslim idea of heaven makes this clear. It presupposes that males enjoy eating good food and having relations with virgins. For many males in our world, that may be the case. However, the Scriptures are quite clear that having relations with virgins (plural) is wrong. The age to come is not a place where God's commandments suddenly change, so that what is sinful in this age will no longer be sinful in the age to come. In fact, we as Christians look forward to the return of Jesus and life in the new heavens and the new earth because they spell the final, ultimate death and destruction of our sinful natures. No longer will we be sinners who have been sainted in the waters of Baptism; instead, we will be saints through and through, without any taint of sinfulness. We will no longer desire what is contrary to God's Law.

Of course, debunking the Muslim idea of heaven on the basis of Scripture is pretty easy. However, it may not be so easy to debunk the idea that you can eat rich, chocolaty foods all day without gaining weight or that your twelve-year-old can play video games all day in the age to come or that the avid fisherman can spend all day on the boat. Eating chocolates, playing video games, and fishing are not in and of themselves sinful. Nevertheless, the mistake in thinking still holds. Just because I enjoy dark chocolate squares in this life does not mean I will enjoy them in the life to come. Perhaps the Lord will not provide them in the new heavens and the new earth, or perhaps it will turn out that other joys prove far more appealing in the age to come than eating chocolates. I cannot simply take my earthly desires and project them into the age to come as if that is what heaven will be like. Doing so makes me the measure of heaven.

And that, perhaps, is the greatest problem with the way we tend to talk about heaven. We focus on the place, on the pleasures, on the pets and people we would like to see again rather than focusing on the three persons in one Godhead who form the source and center of heaven. Notice that the Muslim idea of heaven, the preteen idea of heaven, and even the fisherman's idea of heaven make no reference to God. They take no account of the words spoken to John, that the Lamb's "servants will worship Him" (Revelation 22:3). In the end, what we call heaven is about face-to-face communion with the Lord God Almighty who created us, the Lamb who redeemed us, and the Spirit who sanctified us. The Scriptures certainly suggest that other activities will fill our time in the age to come as well. Isaiah (25:6) speaks of "a feast of rich food, a feast of well-aged wine, of rich food full of marrow, of aged wine well refined." Jesus likens the age to come to a wedding feast (Matthew 25:10). The apostle John had visions of the kings of the earth bringing their glory into the holy city (Revelation 21:24), and Isaiah writes, (60:5, 11) "Then you shall see and be radiant; your heart shall thrill and exult, because the abundance of the sea shall be turned to you, the wealth of the nations shall come to you. . . . Your gates shall be open continually; day and night they shall not be shut, that people may bring to you the wealth of the nations, with their kings led in procession." In other words, the age to come may not be a perpetual worship service. However, if there is feasting in the kingdom of heaven, it is feasting at the table of God in celebration of the Church's marriage to the Lamb who was slain. If the wealth of the nations is literally brought into the Holy City Jerusalem, it is to honor the God who redeemed all humanity and created the new heavens and the new earth. If there is "life outside of worship" in the age to come, it will still be life with God.

2 Walking by the Spirit

What we have learned so far might leave our preteens wondering whether they will enjoy heaven after all. If they do not get to enjoy in the age to come what they enjoy here, what will be left? However, the concern that life in the age to come will be boring is just the flip side of the idea that we will get to do in the age to come whatever we like to do here. The thinking goes something like this: (1) There will be worship in heaven; (2) I find worship boring; so (3) I will find heaven boring. The mistake lies in the move from statement 2 to statement 3. It is not necessarily true that what we find boring in this life we will also find boring in the life to come. Ask yourself for a moment what makes worship boring for a preteen (or an adult, for that matter). First, there's the sermon (the preached Word of God). It is perhaps too long for the attention span of your typical twelve-year-old, or it deals with topics that are not really troubling to the preteen, or it is just "not dynamic." Then there is the music, which is for the most part composed not to entertain but to convey a message or to express a prayer. Then there are the prayers of the church. The author of this study has to confess that he dreaded the prayers of the church when he was growing up, because he found them (you guessed it) long and boring. He could not concentrate long enough to follow along.

All of these issues are bound up with our sinful existence in this life. God tells us in the Third Commandment to keep the Sabbath Day holy, which means, "We should fear and love God so that we do not despise preaching and His Word, but hold it sacred and gladly hear and learn it" (Luther's Small Catechism, Third Commandment). God tells us in the Second Commandment not to misuse His name, and the catechism reminds us that using God's name properly includes praying to Him in every trouble. In other words, it is a sin to find God's Word boring, and it is a sin to let your mind wander from prayer. Thank God that His Son, Jesus, not only took our sins away by dying on the cross but also fulfilled the Second and Third Commandments for us by learning God's Word and praying regularly. Because He has redeemed us from the curse of the Law and fulfilled the Law for us, we will receive the inheritance of life in the age to come.

If we are to appreciate the promise of heaven fully, we must come face-to-face with the depth of our sin in this life. Paul wrote words that should be hauntingly familiar to every Christian, because every Christian has sinful desires against which he or she must struggle. For some, those desires are sexual; for others, they are related to anger; for yet others, they may have to do with money (greed), food (gluttony), possessions (envy), or other areas of life. Paul wrote: (Romans 7:15–19)

> For I do not understand my own actions. For I do not do what I want, but I do the very thing I hate. Now if I do what I do not want, I agree with the law, that it is good. So now it is no longer I who do it, but sin that dwells within me. For I know that nothing good dwells in me, that is, in my flesh. For I have the desire to do what is right, but not the ability to carry it out. For I do not do the good I want, but the evil I do not want is what I keep on doing.

The apostle James likewise recognized that the fights and quarrels among human beings flow from the sinful desires within the heart of each person: (4:1) "What causes quarrels and what causes fights among you? Is it not this, that your passions are at war within you?" The apostle Peter admonishes believers, (1 Peter 2:11) "Beloved, I urge you as sojourners and exiles to abstain from the passions of the flesh, which wage war against your soul." The passions of the flesh are all those evil desires with which each Christian struggles.

We live with these sinful desires in this life. Baptism washes away your sins—that is, in Baptism God cleanses you of your guilt for the sake of our Savior Jesus. Baptism makes you a child of God and a co-heir with Christ, and it turns you into a saint. It does not, however, destroy the sinful desires within you (what Paul and Peter call "the flesh," and what the catechism calls "the sinful nature"). As Paul so vividly described, we Christians still struggle against that sinful self. We struggle against it by confessing our sins and hearing God's absolution (both in the Scriptures and from the mouth of the pastor). We struggle against it by receiving the body and blood of our Savior, Jesus, in the Sacrament of the Altar. We struggle against it by saying no to our sinful desires and setting our minds on things above. We seek the Spirit's strength to "keep in step with the Spirit" (Galatians 5:25) through the good news of forgiveness conveyed in God's Word and in Baptism. When we do so, we confess with Paul that God's Law is good. The problem is not with God's Law; it is with us. God's Law simply lays out what love looks like—how human creatures embody love toward God and toward one another in their lives. The problem is that we fail to love God with all our heart and soul and might; we fail to fear, love, and trust in God above all things. We fail, because the sinful nature is still part of our lives.

Bodily death means the end of the sinful nature for Christians, and the second coming of Christ means the destruction of the sinful nature for Christians. Once the sinful nature meets its final, ultimate defeat and destruction through Jesus Christ, then all that is left of us Christians is the new creation, the saint that was created in Baptism. We will then be all saint and in no way sinner. We will fear, love, and trust in God above all things. We will enjoy whatever gifts He gives without letting the gifts overshadow the giver. We will find joy in our communion with God—both in hearing Him speak to us and in speaking back to Him. We will be changed in such a way that we will never find worship boring, even if life in the age to come should consist of a perpetual worship service. We will be changed such that we will always enjoy whatever activities God asks us to do, even if we do not enjoy those activities in this life. We will be changed so that we no longer experience God's Law as a negative force telling us, "Stop that" or "Start doing this." Instead, God's Law will animate our actions so that we spontaneously live out love toward God and toward one another. As the Lord said through Jeremiah, (30:22) "You shall be My people, and I will be your God."

None of this helps us to know for certain what we will or will not do in heaven. In fact, it actually adds to our uncertainty. After all, just because I enjoy something (sinful or not) in this life does not mean I will do it in the life to come, and just because I find something boring in this life does not mean it will not take place in the life to come. In short, my earthly desires and ideas do not decide what heaven will be like. God decides. God, however, is a loving and merciful God. He is the one who created us with bodies and minds and souls and memories and spirits and the need for relationships. He is the one who will raise us from the dust of the earth to live with Him forever in the new heaven and the new earth. He will give us only what is good in the life to come. Moreover, in the life to come, we will want only the good God has given us. What we have and what we want will come into perfect harmony.

It therefore takes two statements to describe our state in the life to come. We will have everything we want, and we will want only what God has given us. If you leave off the second statement, then you are describing a heaven that is just this life on steroids. If you put both statements together, however, you are describing a state of perfect communion between us and God—a state in which we rejoice in and enjoy everything God gives us and cannot even imagine wanting anything else. We will have everything we want in the life to come, and we will want only what God has given us.

Conclusion

The last session began with the beautiful words of the Revelation to John: (21:3) "Behold, the dwelling place of God is with man. He will dwell with them, and they will be His people, and God Himself will be with them as their God." These words repeat what God has promised through the prophets in the Old Testament: that God is wholly devoted to us, and that we will one day be wholly devoted to Him. (Jeremiah 31:33) "This is the covenant that I will make with the house of Israel after those days, declares the LORD: I will put My law within them, and I will write it on their hearts. And I will be their God, and they shall be My people." God's people will no longer wander after false gods. We will no longer desire what is sinful. We will no longer wish for more than God has given us. We will be a people entirely, wholly devoted to God. Because He is good, He will give us everything we need for eternal joy and pleasure, and because we will be His people, we will rejoice in everything He gives us without wanting more.

This helps answer questions about our relationship to loved ones in heaven. The Scriptures do not say whether we will have heightened attachments to particular people in heaven. They neither affirm nor deny that we will feel closer to those who in this life are parents, spouses, children, siblings, and such. They do say that we will have perfect communion with God, which means that we will rejoice in and enjoy everything He gives us. If the Lord permits us to maintain special relationships in the age to come, then we will rejoice in those relationships. If not, then we will still rejoice in God's gifts. Either way, my relationship with other people will never interfere with my communion with God, and my communion with God will never feel like it draws me away from other gifts that God has given me. There will be no tension in heaven between golf and church or sleeping in and hearing God speak. This likewise helps to answer questions about our attitude toward those in hell. As we saw in the previous session, people in the new heavens and the new earth may well be aware of the torment of people in hell. To our sensibilities now, this seems most difficult to swallow. However, in the end, the Lord will change us so that we rejoice in His mercy toward us and in His justice toward those who remain unrepentant against Him. In particular, the Lord will somehow wipe away the tears we shed for loved ones who continue to reject Him, and we will no longer feel the pain we feel for them in this life. How that will be, we cannot say, but we must simply leave it in the hands of our gracious God, who in His mercy has redeemed us from hell and given us the promise of everlasting joy at His right hand. In the end, we will have everything we want, even if we do not then have everything that we want now. In the end, we will be God's people, wholly devoted to Him.

Concluding Activities

Speak a closing prayer, make any necessary announcements, and distribute study leaflet 8.

"For the Healing of the Nations"

Selected Passages

Preparing for the Session

Central Focus

Life in this age is filled with conflict, but in the new heavens and the new earth, we will enjoy perfect peace, because the tree of life will grow there, and "the leaves of the tree were for the healing of the nations" (Revelation 22:2).

Objectives

That participants, led by the Holy Spirit working through God's Word, will

1. understand conflict (interpersonal and international) as a symptom of human sinfulness;
2. seek reconciliation in the power of the Spirit;
3. rejoice in the great diversity of the church on earth; and
4. look with longing for the perfect peace of the age to come.

Note for the small-group leaders: Lesson notes and other materials you will need begin on page 71.

For the Lecture Leader

Session Plan

Worship

Begin the session with the hymn printed in the study leaflet. Accompaniments are available in denominational hymnals, such as *Lutheran Service Book* or *Lutheran Worship* (refer to hymnal index). (Note: Concordia Publishing House has available *The Concordia Organist*, a 31-CD collection of pipe organ accompaniments for all the hymns and liturgical music in *Lutheran Service Book*. All the initial worship hymns in the LifeLight courses are included in this resource. It's especially helpful for mission congregations and small parishes. See the list of study resources on p. 7.) Follow with this prayer:

Prayer

Heavenly Father, God of all concord, it is Your gracious will that Your children on earth live together in harmony and peace. Defeat the plans of all those who would stir up violence and strife, destroy the weapons of those who delight in war and bloodshed, and, according to Your will, end all conflicts in the world. Teach us to examine our hearts that we may recognize our own inclination toward envy, malice, hatred, and enmity. Help us, by Your Word and Spirit, to search our hearts and to root out the evil that would lead to strife and discord, so that in our lives we may be at peace with all people. Fill us with zeal for the work of Your Church and the proclamation of the Gospel of Jesus Christ, which alone can bring that peace which is beyond all understanding; through Jesus Christ, our Lord. Amen. (*LSB Altar Book;* p. 454)

Lecture Presentation

Introduction

One struggle in writing a Bible study like LifeLight is to make it concrete enough that participants can identify with examples in their own lives, but also generic enough that it will not be outdated in a year or two. This is easy for a session about conflict. If you live or work with other people, you are well aware that our lives are full of interpersonal conflict. When it comes to international conflict, the situation is no different. Nations are constantly posturing and positioning to gain influence and prestige in the so-called international community. Borders between some nations have been disputed for decades. The United States was directly involved in one or more wars or armed conflicts in every decade of the twentieth century, and the twenty-first century has not started off any differently. One beautiful promise of the age to come is that all these conflicts will finally stand behind us. Living in the presence of the Lamb who reconciled us to the Father, believers of "every nation and tribe and language and people" will be fully reconciled with one another (Revelation 14:6). We will live in peace.

1 Cain, Babel, and Geopolitical Turmoil

The first recorded murder in the Bible is Cain's murder of Abel. (Genesis 4:2–5) "Abel was a keeper of sheep, and Cain a worker of the ground. In the course of time Cain brought to the LORD an offering of the fruit of the ground, and Abel also brought of the firstborn of his flock and of their fat portions. And the LORD had regard for Abel and his offering, but for Cain and his offering He had no regard. So Cain was very angry, and his face fell." In his anger, Cain then killed his brother in cold blood. The apostle John tells us, (1 John 3:12) "We should not be like Cain, who was of the evil one and murdered his brother. And why did he murder him? Because his own deeds were evil and his brother's righteous." Cain offered his sacrifice to God, but in offering his sacrifice, he nevertheless violated God's will for how we relate to Him. He sinned against God, and his distance from God translated into distance from his brother Abel. Broken communion with God led—and leads—to broken relationships with our fellow human beings.

We see the evidence of these broken relationships already in the Garden of Eden. God had created Eve as a helper for Adam. The two of them were to tend the garden, raise children, and worship God together. Yet as soon as the two of them ate of the fruit of the tree of the knowledge of good and evil, their perfect partnership fell to pieces. God went looking for them, and they felt their distance from God, so they hid. Then, when God found them and took Adam to task for violating His express command not to eat of the fruit of that tree, Adam responded, (Genesis 3:12) "The woman whom You gave to be with me, she gave me fruit of the tree, and I ate." Instead of trying teamwork, Adam plays the blame game. He is aware that he violated God's Word, so he feels alienated from God. In his alienation from God, he breaks his relationship with his wife as well.

This pattern of alienation from God and broken relationships with fellow human beings is repeated again and again in the history of God's people recorded in the Scriptures, and it is repeated again and again in our own lives. Even Christians, who have been reconciled to the Father through the death of Jesus Christ, end up in conflict with one another. Thankfully, the forgiveness we have through Jesus Christ permits us to be reconciled to one another as well. In the church, we strive to live without broken relationships, but we must also understand that we are still sinners. This side of heaven, our anger, pride, self-protection, and insecurity will get the better of us and lead us to treat one another poorly. That is sin, plain and simple. (Colossians 3:8) "You must put them all away: anger, wrath, malice, slander, and obscene talk from your mouth." Praise God, however, that His Church is the fellowship of sinners reconciled to the Father through the sacrifice of Jesus Christ, because people who have been reconciled to the Father are able to be reconciled to one another as well. We do not need to handle our conflicts the way the rest of the world does. Instead, we can confess our wrongdoings, intentional and unintentional, forgive one another, and experience a foretaste of that perfect peace that will be ours in the age to come.

Of course, interpersonal peace is not the only kind of peace for which we long. We also long for peace at the international level. A traditional Christian prayer going back over a thousand years gives voice to that longing: "Give peace in our time, O Lord." The seeds of geopolitical turmoil and international conflict were planted at the same time as the seeds of interpersonal conflict, but it took one more event to put us into today's position. Genesis 11 recounts how the all people of the earth after the great flood lived in one place and spoke one language. (Genesis 11:4) "They said, 'Come, let us build ourselves a city and a tower with its top in the heavens, and let us make a name for ourselves, lest we be dispersed over the face of the whole earth.'" Now here is the question: if there was only one nation under heaven at the time, with whom were the people trying to make a name for themselves? This was not like the space race, in which two nations rushed to put a man in orbit in order to make a name among all the other nations. At the time of the Tower of Babel, there were no other nations in the world. The only other person with whom the people building that tower might hope to make a name for themselves was none other than God. The people had developed such pride that they wanted to climb a tower to heaven, pull a chair up next to God, and say to Him, "See, we're powerful too, just like You." You know the rest of the story. After they had built the tower far into the heavens, God looked down (notice—He was still so far above them that He had to look down), saw what they were doing, and then went down (notice—as high as they had built, He still had to come down to them). He confused their languages. This event marks the birth of a divided humanity. We are no longer one people, but many peoples speaking different languages. We are no longer one tribe working together to achieve some immense goal; we are multiple tribes often pitted against one another. Although God's intervention brought the end of that particular project, it did not bring the end of our human pride. The same kind of pride that led the people to believe they could make a name for themselves with God leads tribes and peoples and nations and races in our day to believe that one is somehow better than others. Unfortunately, racism is still rampant in our nation and around the world to this day.

And then there are wars.

While the church has often become a tool of human pride by reinforcing these distinctions and rivalries, the church has also often provided an amazing picture of reconciliation. Two stories illustrate both points. One is apocryphal, although it surely contains an element of truth. It was the 1950s or 1960s, and a young African American man had come to attend the Lutheran college in a Midwestern town. He had been baptized and confirmed in the Lutheran church where he was raised. Naturally, he sought out the Lutheran church in his temporary home, and his presence stirred up quite a discussion among the people of the parish, all of whom were white and many of whom had never actually met an African American person. The voters' assembly finally passed a resolution thanking God that the young African American man was Lutheran but declaring that he ought to find another Lutheran church in which to worship. Their action was a sin, to be sure—not because our own day of political correctness says so, but because the Scriptures declare, (Galatians 3:28) "There is neither Jew nor Greek, there is neither slave nor free, there is no male and female, for you are all one in Christ Jesus." The people of this congregation based fellowship on something besides confession of the faith, and at the same time, they simply fell flat in showing the world the picture of heaven that was revealed to John: (Revelation 7:9–10) "A great multitude that no one could number, from every nation, from all tribes and peoples and languages, standing before the throne and before the Lamb, clothed in white robes, with palm branches in their hands, and crying out with a loud voice, 'Salvation belongs to our God who sits on the throne, and to the Lamb!'" Thankfully, according to the story, their pastor then stood up and told them that no one in the congregation would receive the Lord's Supper until the young man was welcome to do so. It was a bygone era of strong respect for the pastoral office, and the voters' assembly quickly rescinded its decision and voted to welcome the young man into their midst.

A second example comes from the terrible war between the Hutu and Tutsi peoples in Rwanda. The minority Tutsi had ruled for centuries, until the majority Hutu gained power around 1960. In 1994, tensions between the two ethnic groups erupted into full-blown bloodshed. The Hutu government began a hundred-day campaign to kill the Tutsi as well as pro-peace Hutus; at least one Hutu cabinet member is reported to have said that she was in favor of getting rid of all Tutsi because that would solve all of Rwanda's problems. During that terrible time, somewhere between 500,000 and 1,000,000 people were murdered. However, in the midst of the bloodbath, the girls at one Christian boarding school refused to cooperate when the Hutu militia came and told them to divide themselves into Hutu and Tutsi. The girls—both Hutu and Tusti—paid with their lives. They died for the confession that they were one in Christ despite their ethnic differences. Their actions were a living example of that old Sunday School song "Jesus loves the little children, all the children of the world. Red and yellow, black and white, They are precious in His sight. Jesus loves the little children of the world." In their actions, they gave a small foreshadowing of the beautiful diversity we will enjoy in the new heavens and the new earth, a diversity that will be reconciled into unity through the Lamb who was slain.

2 The Healing of the Nations

Many passages in the Scriptures point forward to this time of wonderful unity among believers of every tribe and language and people and nation. The visions begin in the Old Testament. To take one beautiful example, Isaiah and Micah both write:

> (Isaiah 2:2–4; see Micah 4:1–3) It shall come to pass in the latter days that the mountain of the house of the Lord shall be established as the highest of the mountains, and shall be lifted up above the hills; and all the nations shall flow to it, and many peoples shall come, and say: "Come, let us go up to the mountain of the Lord, to the house of the God of Jacob, that He may teach us His ways and that we may walk in His paths." For out of Zion shall go the law, and the Word of the Lord from Jerusalem. He shall judge between the nations, and shall decide disputes for many peoples; and they shall beat their swords into plowshares, and their spears into pruning hooks; nation shall not lift up sword against nation, neither shall they learn war anymore.

Isaiah and Micah were both writing to the people of Judah (the Southern Kingdom, ruled by descendants of King David). The kings and people of the Southern Kingdom had abandoned faith in the one true God and worshiped a variety of idols. At the same time, they found themselves threatened by a variety of foreign nations: the Northern Kingdom (the ten tribes of Israel that had broken away), Syria (or Aram), the superpower Assyria, and a variety of smaller nations on their various borders. It was a tremendous irony that they lost faith in the very God who had claimed them as His chosen people and instead worshiped the idols of the same surrounding nations that were now threatening them. Isaiah and Micah point out the irony by revealing a day when all the nations of the earth will abandon their idols and instead seek the Lord God Almighty. What is more, the people of Judah will have the peace for which they long only when they and all nations seek the Lord. On that day, "they shall beat their swords into plowshares, and their spears into pruning hooks" (Isaiah 2:4; Micah 1:3). In the age to come, when the believers of all the nations are gathered into one place to seek the Lord and hear His Word, their pride will give way to humility before God, so wars will cease to the ends of the earth (Psalm 46:9).

Jesus makes a similar point when a Roman centurion comes and asks Him to heal his servant. The Romans were, of course, Gentiles, and their army was occupying Israel. The centurion was an officer in the Roman army, so he had two strikes against him. Nevertheless, when he came to Jesus with his request, Jesus was amazed at his faith. Jesus then said, (Matthew 8:11–12) "I tell you, many will come from east and west and recline at table with Abraham, Isaac, and Jacob in the kingdom of heaven, while the sons of the kingdom will be thrown into the outer darkness. In that place there will be weeping and gnashing of teeth." "Sons of the kingdom" refers to the Israelites, many of whom rejected Jesus. The "many [who] will come from east and west" are the people of other nations who will come and join believing Israelites in the kingdom of heaven. While Jesus' imagery is not as vivid to us as that of the prophets, He nevertheless affirmed that heaven will be filled with people from every tribe and nation, not simply with Jews. He makes the same point in Luke 13:28. The apostle Paul builds on Jesus' words when He tells the Gentiles in Ephesus not to look down on the Jewish Christians: (Ephesians 2:14–16) "For He Himself is our peace, who has made us both one and has broken down in His flesh the dividing wall of hostility by abolishing the law of commandments expressed in ordinances, that He might create in Himself one new man in place of the two, so making peace, and might reconcile us both to God in one body through the cross, thereby killing the hostility."

In Revelation, John likewise bears witness to the everlasting peace that will be ours in the age to come. He writes, (22:1–2) "Then the angel showed me the river of the water of life, bright as crystal, flowing from the throne of God and of the Lamb through the middle of the street of the city; also, on either side of the river, the tree of life with its twelve kinds of fruit, yielding its fruit each month. The leaves of the tree were for the healing of the nations." From the throne of God flows the water of life, and the water of life nourishes the tree of life, from which God banished humankind when He exiled us from the Garden of Eden because of our disobedience. The tree bears not just one kind of fruit but twelve kinds of fruit (the same number as the tribes of Israel, as a reminder that God has grafted Gentiles into the people of Israel to give Abraham descendants as numerous as the stars in the sky and the sand on the beach). Moreover, John writes, the leaves of the tree are for the healing of the nations. The wounds we have inflicted upon one another, the anger we have provoked in one another, the pride we have shown over one another—it will all be healed by the leaves of that tree, which is sustained by the water of life flowing from the throne of God and the Lamb. Prideful humanity, divided by God at Babel, is humbled through God's Law, and through the sacrifice of the Lamb we are raised up and reconciled into the one Body of Christ. The divisions we brought on ourselves, God heals; and He will unite us as one people in the age to come.

Some thinkers through the ages have postulated that a lasting, worldwide peace could be achieved if certain conditions were met. The philosopher Immanuel Kant suggested that the spread of republican governments, coupled with significant international trade, might eventually clear away the conditions that lead to war. More recently, some American and European philosophers have argued that greater economic equality among nations would reduce the hatred that many Middle Eastern cultures have toward the West. These thinkers may be correct that a radical change in the political and economic structures of our world would reduce or completely do away with war, but they fail to understand that human beings are incorrigibly sinful and therefore incorrigibly prideful. Thus, even if radical political and economic change could end war (and that is a big *if*), and even if we were able to understand politics and economics well enough to make such a radical change (which is also a big *if*), even then the pride, greed, avarice, and general self-centeredness of sinful human beings would make it impossible to bring the vast majority of humanity along. That is why every attempt at utopia—every attempt at creating a perfect society without friction—has either failed miserably or been limited to a small community of people. Mere political and economic change cannot end war, because ending war requires nothing less than a radical change in the human heart. Humankind cannot work that change in ourselves. That change must come from outside of us.

It is precisely this change that the Holy Spirit works in us who believe in Jesus Christ. (Colossians 1:21–23) "You, who once were alienated and hostile in mind, doing evil deeds, He [Jesus] has now reconciled in His body of flesh by His death, in order to present you holy and blameless and above reproach before Him, if indeed you continue in the faith, stable and steadfast, not shifting from the hope of the gospel that you heard, which has been proclaimed in all creation under heaven." (2 Corinthians 3:18) "We all, with unveiled face, beholding the glory of the Lord, are being transformed into the same image from one degree of glory to another. For this comes from the Lord who is the Spirit." Our Lord Jesus reconciled us to the Father through His death on the cross, and the good news of this reconciliation transforms us into the image of Christ, so that we, like our Savior, reach out to be reconciled to others. Our nature is changed. (2 Corinthians 5:17) "If anyone is in Christ, he is a new creation. The old has passed away; behold, the new has come." In the new heavens and the new earth, when our old, sinful natures have been destroyed with this creation, we will finally be without any of the old pride and anger that led Cain to murder Abel, that led the people to build a tower up to heaven at Babel, and that led one nation to raise swords against another nation. We will eat the leaves of the tree of life, and all our divisions will be healed. On that day, what is only prefigured and foreshadowed in Christian churches around the world will be a glorious reality: people from every tribe and language and people and nation will join their voices in praising the Lord God Almighty.

Conclusion

Will there be conflict in heaven? Maybe or maybe not—but if there is, it will never lead to broken relationships, we will always resolve it in perfect love toward one another, and it will always be productive. What we now know as conflict, however—the painful breaches in our relationships with friends and family and the destructive aggression of one people and nation against another—will have no place in the age to come. Instead of the pride we have in this life, we will have humility toward God. Instead of the anger we have in this life, we will have love toward one another. Instead of the swords and spears we have in this life, we will have plowshares and pruning hooks, and we will drink from the water of life, and we will eat from the tree of life, and its leaves will heal the nations.

Concluding Activities

Speak a closing prayer, make any necessary announcements, and distribute study leaflet 9.

Living Heavenward

Selected Passages

Preparing for the Session

Central Focus

The hope of heaven does not draw our attention away from this life. Rather, it sustains us in this life and moves us to share the Good News with others so they may also enjoy everlasting life with God.

Objectives

That participants, led by the Holy Spirit working through God's Word, will

1. embrace their earthly vocations as signs of God's love toward the world;
2. seek to prefigure the peace of heaven in their relationships;
3. learn to live in hope of the age to come; and
4. develop strategies to share the good news of heaven with others.

Note for the small-group leaders: Lesson notes and other materials you will need begin on page 73.

For the Lecture Leader

Session Plan

Worship

Begin the session with the hymn printed in the study leaflet. Accompaniments are available in denominational hymnals, such as *Lutheran Service Book* or *Lutheran Worship* (refer to hymnal index). (Note: Concordia Publishing House has available *The Concordia Organist*, a 31-CD collection of pipe organ accompaniments for all the hymns and liturgical music in *Lutheran Service Book*. All the initial worship hymns in the LifeLight courses are included in this resource. It's especially helpful for mission congregations and small parishes. See the list of study resources on p. 7.) Follow with this prayer:

Prayer

Almighty and everlasting God, through Your Son You have promised us forgiveness of sins and everlasting life. Govern our hearts by Your Holy Spirit that in our daily need, and especially in all time of temptation, we may seek Your help and, by a true and lively faith in Your Word, obtain all that Your have promised; through the same Jesus Christ, our Lord. Amen. (*LSB Altar Book;* p. 451)

Lecture Presentation

Introduction

Christians have long been accused of having our heads so wrapped up in heaven that we do not take good care of people in this life. This accusation is pure hogwash. The fact is that being Christians, because we long for and look for the revelation of Jesus Christ, we throw ourselves into daily life in this world with great confidence and vigor. The first real hospitals were opened by Christians. Christians cared for orphans when many others simply abandoned them. Christian men and women have risen early in the morning to scratch out a living for their families from the earth. Heaven is not an escape from this world for Christians. It is the hope that sustains us in our vocations in this world, and it is a hope we share with others.

1 The Christian in this World

In the early years of Christianity and into the medieval period, some Christians thought that life in the "normal" world somehow kept one from having a close communion with God. Men and women who wanted closer communion with God would forsake the ordinary world—owning and managing property, marrying, raising children, and the like—to devote themselves to more spiritual callings. These were the monks and nuns. People actually believed that monks and nuns did the spiritual work of the community, while ordinary people did the earthly work. If you needed a prayer said, you paid the monks to say the prayers for you. If you needed meat, you paid a butcher to cut if for you.

That way of life has pretty well disappeared from the Western world. However, the theological bias behind it has not. Christians still sometimes talk as if the mundane, messy life of this world has no real connection to our communion with God. There are even some Christians who find it difficult to explain why they should not read their Bibles or pray all the time, even if their devotional time interrupts work or family responsibilities. Others feel guilty when they take time to enjoy life, as if time spent in recreation is time taken away from communion with God. Still others leave perfectly acceptable "ordinary" jobs to start or work in "ministries" so they can become more "spiritual." (If you think working in a ministry, such as a congregation, a church school, or Christian organization, will make you more spiritual, you should talk to your pastor or another church worker. You may be surprised by what you hear. There are good reasons to work for a church or church-related institution, but being more spiritual is not one of them.)

If God had intended for everyone to spend all day, every day in worship, He would have told the Israelites never to work. Instead, He told them to take one day away from their work to worship Him. The Old Testament knows no tension between spiritual and earthly activities. God set apart one group of people to care for the worship space, but they were not any more spiritual than the other people. He even set apart another group to conduct ceremonies and rituals, but their work was not more important than that of the others. After all, the ceremonies and rituals called for cattle and sheep and goats. They called for grain and olive oil and wine. Without people to tend the animals and cultivate the plants, there would be no materials for the rituals, and there would be no food for anyone to eat. What made people "spiritual" was that they trusted the God who had created them, given them their various skills, provided for them, and would ultimately redeem them through the blood of the final sacrifice, Jesus Christ. They were holy because the Lord God chose to dwell among them. He told them, (Deuteronomy 7:6) "You are a people holy to the LORD your God. The LORD your God has chosen you to be a people for His treasured possession, out of all the peoples who are on the face of the earth." It was not their occupations that made them more or less holy or more or less spiritual. It was the fact that God the Father had chosen and redeemed them. When they went out to till the land and care for the animals, they did so as God's holy people fulfilling His command to "be fruitful and multiply and fill the earth and subdue it" (Genesis 1:28). They did so as God's holy people who had the privilege of participating in God's blessing of the earth to provide for all people.

The same holds true today. Prayer is an important part of the Christian life, but a Christian's life should not consist entirely of prayer. Hearing God's Word is an indispensable part of the Christian life, but a Christian's life should not consist entirely of hearing God's Word. There are children to be raised, people who need to buy food, fire victims who need new houses built, sick who need to be cared for, students who need to be taught, civilians who need to be protected, and cities that need to be governed. Riding a garbage truck around all day removing people's trash is no less holy or spiritual than serving as a pastor, because "Jesus also suffered outside the gate in order to sanctify [that is, make holy] the people through His own blood" (Hebrews 13:12). We gather for worship, and we take time for devotions and prayer, but we do so because "man does not live by bread alone, but man lives by every word that comes from the mouth of the LORD" (Deuteronomy 8:3). The Word of God sustains us as we go about our ordinary, everyday, mundane, sometimes messy lives doing the work God has called us to do. We work because God calls us to, and we work to participate in God's blessing of the earth to provide for all people. As Christians who look forward to heaven, we do not lose sight of our neighbors in this life. In fact, because God has shown such great mercy to us through His Son, Jesus, we reflect His mercy to others by caring and providing for them in our various roles in life—whether in the family, in the community, at work, or even at church. (Colossians 3:23–24) "Whatever you do, work heartily, as for the Lord and not for men, knowing that from the Lord you will receive the inheritance as your reward. You are serving the Lord Christ."

Looking forward to life in the age to come does not distract us from life in this age. In fact, the knowledge that we will rise from the dead and live in God's presence forever sustains us in this life. Paul wrote, (Romans 8:18) "I consider that the sufferings of this present time are not worth comparing with the glory that is to be revealed to us." Likewise, Peter proclaimed, (1 Peter 1:3, 6) "Blessed be the God and Father of our Lord Jesus Christ! According to His great mercy, He has caused us to be born again to a living hope through the resurrection of Jesus Christ from the dead, . . . though now for a little while, if necessary, you have been grieved by various trials." Even Revelation, filled with scary imagery and difficult passages, was written to encourage

Christians who were facing persecution. We can apply these statements to all the difficulties we face in life, including those in our occupations. John the Baptist did just that. After he had preached a rousing sermon on the coming judgment, people of various professions asked him, (Luke 3:10) "What then shall we do?" John did not tell them to leave their jobs in order to work for ministries. To the tax collectors he said, (v. 13) "Collect no more than you are authorized to do," and to the soldiers he said, (v. 14) "Do not extort money from anyone by threats or by false accusation, and be content with your wages." Whatever we experience in this life, we experience as God's holy children, and whatever we do in this life, we do as God's holy children. The knowledge that we are working with and for the Lord when we carry out our vocations as parent, grandparent, employer, employee, business owner, farmer, or volunteer helps us get through the difficult times in our various vocations. We live out these vocations without fear of messing up and ending up in hell, because the blood of Jesus has washed away our sins. Heaven is ours through faith in Jesus Christ despite our sins, so we can carry out our vocations in confidence of the life to come.

2 Eyes toward Heaven

Even as we live with an eye toward the needs of our neighbors, we also live with an eye toward heaven. Jesus said, (Luke 21:34) "Watch yourselves lest your hearts be weighed down with dissipation and drunkenness and cares of this life, and that day come upon you suddenly like a trap." In Revelation, He said, (16:15) "Behold, I am coming like a thief! Blessed is the one who stays awake, keeping his garments on, that he may not go about naked and be seen exposed!" Peter wrote, (2 Peter 3:11) "Since all these things are thus to be dissolved, what sort of people ought you to be in lives of holiness and godliness." To use that old but still helpful Lutheran lingo, the Judgment Day of Christ functions, in part, as Law. The coming of Jesus and the eternal punishments of hell serve as a constant reminder that our actions in this life have consequences in the age to come. We cannot simply go on living in evil and say, (Psalm 94:7) "The Lord does not see; the God of Jacob does not perceive." When pastors preach about the fires of hell and the impending Day of Judgment, it is in part to keep our eyes focused on the age to come. It is to keep us from growing complacent. It is to call us back from the guilt of our sinful lives to repentance and forgiveness in Christ. We need to hear about God's judgment and about hell itself every so often, so "that we might not desire evil" (1 Corinthians 10:6).

On the other hand, the great glories that God has promised in the age to come keep us going when pain and suffering mount up. The devil knows that his greatest strategy is to keep our eyes so focused on this world and its troubles that we lose heart. That is why Luther explained the Sixth Petition of the Lord's Prayer by saying, "We pray in this petition that God would guard and keep us so that the devil, the world, and our sinful nature may not deceive us or mislead us into false belief, despair, and other great shame and vice" (Small Catechism). It will not be our sins that keep us out of heaven, but our lack of faith in Christ or despair over God's ability to redeem us from all the troubles of this life. The devil knows this, and so he does his best to point out what is going poorly in this world. You have been diagnosed with cancer, and you still have young children living at home. Your mother, with whom you had been so close, has forgotten who you are because of Alzheimer's, and it is just not fair. Your spouse, with whom you had dreamed of building a life and enjoying retirement, is now living in a different house with a different person, and you find yourself sharing the kids instead of spending time together as a family. Work was a pretty decent place until the new supervisor arrived, and you know that Christians should not think the things you do, but the new supervisor is a jerk, to say the least. Or work was a decent place until the company downsized, and now your meager savings has been drained and you are behind on your house payments. The list could go on. The devil takes these events, and he conspires with your own sinful flesh to raise that age-old question, "How could God let this happen?" Or he simply stands idly by while you find old religious feelings fading and withdraw slowly from the church until it is just easier to sleep away your troubles on Sunday morning rather than face the people at church and explain again how poorly life is going right now.

Our Lord Jesus knows the difficulties we face in this world. He Himself faced them. He faced them and kept the faith on our behalf, so that even when we fail, we are nevertheless completely and fully righteous in the eyes of God through faith in Him. His righteousness is ours, and His fate is ours. (Romans 6:4–5) "We were buried therefore with Him by baptism into death, in order that, just as Christ was raised from the dead by the glory of the Father, we too might walk in newness of life. For if we have been united with Him in a death like

His, we shall certainly be united with Him in a resurrection like His." The crosses we bear in this life as parents, children, employers, employees, neighbors, and fellow Christians are all made holy by the cross of Jesus Christ, and just as the cross was transfigured into an instrument of redemption through the death of Christ, so the crosses we bear will be overcome at the second coming of Christ. We as Christians need to hear not only the Law, but also the Gospel. We need to hear about the glories of heaven. When pastors preach about the joys of the life to come, they lift our eyes above the crosses we are bearing right now to the redemption that Christ has already secured for us. They point beyond the dark, shadowy trail on which we now walk to the bright sunrise on the horizon. They fight off our own sinful flesh and the devil himself with the Word of God. And when they serve us the body and blood of our Savior, Jesus, in the Sacrament of the Altar, they are doing nothing less than giving us a foretaste of the feast to come. They lift our eyes to heaven, so that we can live with hope and joy in this sinful world.

3 Little Pieces of Heaven on Earth

While we live in this world, we have a unique privilege. Our works and our words do not save us, but they may help to save others. Peter wrote, (1 Peter 3:15) "In your hearts honor Christ the Lord as holy, always being prepared to make a defense to anyone who asks you for a reason for the hope that is in you." The Word of God belongs not just to pastors but to every Christian, and every Christian has the joyful privilege of pointing out the joys of everlasting life to unbelievers and to fellow believers. We Christians already live, however imperfectly, the resurrection life, which will be fully realized in us in the age to come. The Church, therefore, foreshadows heaven, and each of us can bring a little piece of heaven to earth.

In the last session, we saw how racial reconciliation among Christians brings a little bit of heaven to earth. We can do the same in our own ordinary lives. (1 Thessalonians 5:13) "Be at peace among yourselves." When Christians work out their differences with love and respect, we confess before the world that heaven will be a place of peace and unity. When Christians reconcile with one another after fighting, we confess before the world that heaven will be a place where former enemies are now fully reconciled in Christ. When Christians extend forgiveness to unbelievers, we show that our gracious God extends forgiveness to all sinners so that they can live with Him forever in heaven. When Christians love our enemies and do good to those who hate us, we give glory to the God who will do good to us by giving us everlasting life despite all our sins against Him. In the words of Jesus, (Matthew 5:16) "Let your light shine before others, so that they may see your good works and give glory to your Father who is in heaven."

This is difficult work. Some people are simply difficult to get along with. Others refuse to be reconciled, and still others see the offer of forgiveness as a sign of weakness. Thank God that He put in the difficult work to reconcile us to Himself. Because He sent His Son to be incarnate as a human being for us, because His Son died on the cross to win forgiveness, and because His Holy Spirit extends forgiveness to every sinner through the Word of God, you and I are now reconciled to God and have a place in heaven. Our failures in this life are forgiven. Our tongues are loosed to sing God's praises, and our hands are set free to serve others as our gracious God has served us. In Christ Jesus, who fulfilled the Law perfectly for us, our every attempt is made holy, and the Lord God even takes our meager good works and uses them to accomplish far more than we can imagine. We are not on our own when it comes to living out heaven here on earth. The Spirit of God dwells in us through His Word, and He lives out the life of Christ through us in the world.

He even gives us words to speak when it comes time to share the good news explicitly. Pastor John Hofius once told this story: Two boys lived next door to each other; one went to church with his family and the other did not. One day, the two boys were playing in the sandbox. The little boy who went to church asked his neighbor, "Do you go to church?" The other boy answered, "No." "Well, you'd better," came the response, "or you'll go to hell." That is not exactly how we suggest doing evangelism, of course, but the fact is that one powerful statement from the mouth of a young boy brought that other family to church—and more important, to faith in Jesus Christ. We Christians have a Word from God that we can speak to those who hard-heartedly and coldly reject God. Unless they repent, they will go to hell. We also have a Word we can speak to those who are hurting, despairing, looking, seeking, and otherwise discouraged by this life. In Christ Jesus, we have "an inheritance that is imperishable, undefiled, and unfading, kept in heaven for" us (1 Peter 1:4). The Lord is not ignoring those who are going through difficulties. Instead, He has promised to deliver them from all the sinfulness of this world and from their own guilt, and to give them everlasting life through Jesus Christ, and He has sent you into their lives to show His loving presence. You may feel you do not know enough about the Bible to share the Good News of everlasting life with someone or to answer their questions and objections, but ultimately, you are simply speaking God's Word, and the Spirit is the one who does the persuading. You know the Bible stories, and you know the Good News, and you know the hope you have for everlasting life. If you can speak, write, sign, text, type, or otherwise communicate, you can share that hope with others. In the end, you may not only share your hope with them here. If they come to faith, you will share eternity with them as well.

Conclusion

Our study of heaven and hell has covered quite a bit of ground. Hopefully, you have come to appreciate more fully the doctrine of hell—that is, the teaching that God will mete out eternal punishment on unbelievers after Jesus comes back to judge the living and the dead. The teaching is a difficult one, but it points to the justice of God by showing that He holds people responsible for sin and by showing that He protects His people from their enemies. Thinking about hell is not pleasant, but the Scriptures are so full of talk about it that we may not simply write it off. Thankfully, the Scriptures also talk about life in the age to come. Life in the age to come will be glorious, because all believers will live face-to-face with our heavenly Father and with the Lamb who was slain to give us everlasting life. Death will be dead, Satan will be subjugated, and we will be free of our sinful flesh. (Revelation 7:17) "For the Lamb in the midst of the throne will be [our] shepherd, and He will guide [us] to springs of living water, and God will wipe away every tear from [our] eyes." (Revelation 22:20) "Amen. Come, Lord Jesus!" Amen.

Concluding Activities

Close with an appropriate prayer, make any necessary closing announcements, and note for participants when the next LifeLight course will begin.

Small-Group Leaders Material

Cover illustration: Art Kirkhoff © Concordia Publishing House

A Guided Tour of Heaven and Hell

Daniel 12:1–3; 2 Peter 3:1–7; 2 Kings 2:1–12; 1 Kings 8:22–53; Deuteronomy 26:15

Preparing for the Session

Central Focus

By nature, each of us deserves eternal punishment for rejecting God and misusing His gifts. Thankfully, His Son, Jesus, opened the door to heaven through His death and resurrection, so that believers can live with Him forever.

Objectives

That participants, led by the Holy Spirit working through God's Word, will

1. gain an overview of what happens to believers after death;
2. gain an overview of what happens to unbelievers after death; and
3. find comfort in God's gracious gift of heaven.

For the Small-Group Leader

Small-Group Discussion Helps

Day 1 • Daniel 12:1–3

1. The two destinations are either everlasting life or shame and everlasting contempt.

2. Those who are wise and turn many to righteousness will shine like stars.

3. Answers will vary. Encourage answers that move away from the idea that heaven is a "place" (it's up there somewhere) to a "person" (it's with God).

4. Answers will vary. As with Question 3, gently guide the participants from thinking in terms of hell as a place to hell as being cast away from God's presence.

Day 2 • 2 Peter 3:1–7

5. The scoffers will be scoffing and mocking, following their sinful desires. They will overlook the fact that the heavens existed long ago from creation.

6. Answers will vary.

7. Answers will vary, but may include that some people think that a place of punishment is contrary to God's love, or that no one will be condemned, or that the implication that we may not be good enough to suit God is offensive.

8. Answers will vary, but may include that knowing that they have salvation means they are not afraid to admit there is a place of punishment or, simply, that the Bible says there is a hell.

9. Answers will vary. Give people time to explain why they agree or disagree.

Day 3 • 2 Kings 2:1–12

10. Elijah was taken to heaven by a whirlwind.

11. In each case, the Lord does something from heaven. The common theme is that the Lord acts from heaven.

12. Again, in each verse, the Lord sits in heaven or acts from heaven.

13. It describes how the Lord reacts in heaven.

14. When 2 Kings 2:1 says God wanted to take Elijah to heaven, it is saying that God wanted to take Elijah to Himself. What we are beginning to see from this and the other passages we have considered is that heaven is not a special place that is located somewhere, but that it is where we will be gathered around the person of God.

Day 4 • 1 Kings 8:22–53

15. Verses 22, 23, 27, 30, 32, 34, 35, 36, 39, 43, 45, 49.

16. The meaning of the word "heaven" in these three verses is different than in the other verses. Verse 23 talks about "heaven above" the earth, so we can see that it is talking about the sky. Verse 27 probably has the same meaning, since it says the highest heavens cannot contain God, but other verses in the Bible say God dwells in heaven. Finally, verse 35 talks about rain coming from heaven, so it may also be referring to the sky.

17. The rest of the verses talk about God hearing the prayers of His people in heaven. In other words, heaven is where God lives and from where He hears His people to save them.

18. Verse 39 explicitly calls heaven God's "dwelling place."

19. Answers will vary. Two main points should emerge: (a) the Bible uses the word "heaven" in two different ways, and (b) heaven is more about God's presence than a particular location.

Day 5 • Deuteronomy 26:15

20. Heaven is where God lives (His "holy habitation").

21. To speak of location is to speak of a place in this visible creation (i.e., the world around us—the heavens and the earth, so to speak). Heaven, however, is not a geographic location.

22. If we understand heaven as the dwelling place of God, from which He acts to save His people, then we are certainly justified in saying that believers go to heaven when they die.

23. Answers will vary, but should center on being gathered into God's saving presence.

24. Going to hell is the exact opposite of going to heaven—it means being sent away from God's saving presence.

"Daddy, What Happens When We Die?"

Matthew 27:45–50; John 19:28–30; 1 Peter 3:18–20; Psalm 49:13–15; 1 Corinthians 15:12–26; Matthew 22:23–33

Preparing for the Session

Central Focus

The Bible has many ways of referring to death, all of which point to our true comfort as Christians: that those who die in the faith rest from their labors in this world and remain safe with Christ until He raises them from the dead to live with Him forever.

Objectives

That participants, led by the Holy Spirit working through God's Word, will

1. understand the distinction between the interim state and the resurrection;
2. explain what Jesus means by referring to death as "sleeping";
3. give a biblical explanation of the interim state of the righteous and the unrighteous; and
4. find comfort in the rest enjoyed by those who die in the faith.

For the Small-Group Leader

Small-Group Discussion Helps

Day 1 • Matthew 27:45–50; John 19:28–30

1. Answers will vary, but most people will likely answer by saying that the soul separates from the body and goes to heaven.

2. In those passages, we read that when Jesus died, He gave up His spirit.

3. A body with its spirit is alive, but a body without its spirit is dead.

4. This passage alludes to death by referring to the removal of the soul from the body.

5. As Christians, our hope is that our Lord Jesus will keep our body, soul, and spirit safe until He comes again to reunite them on the Last Day.

Day 2 • 1 Peter 3:18–20

6. Answers will vary, but some people may say that they go to hell.

7. Their spirits were held in prison.

8. The wicked will go to Sheol after they die. (Although some versions of the Bible translate the Hebrew word as "the grave," there is a different word in Hebrew that refers to a grave in which someone is buried. Other versions translate the word as "hell," but, as the word "hell" is also used to refer to the bodily torment of unbelievers after the resurrection, the Hebrew word here cannot refer to hell in this sense—it is referring to a time prior to the Last Day and the resurrection. Thus the English Standard Version simply transliterates the Hebrew word, which is *Sheol.*)

9. She follows the path to Sheol, so that a man who gives in to her temptations will likewise find himself heading toward Sheol. What we see here is a warning against drifting into seemingly alluring, comfortable, unrepentant sinfulness. A transgression may seem wonderful, or simply harmless, but is in fact something far different—and very dangerous.

10. Sheol is described as a place of weakness and darkness. The spirits in Sheol do not praise God.

Day 3 • Psalm 49:13–15

11. Answers will vary but will probably include some of the following: our souls go to heaven, our souls are gathered to Christ, or we wait for our glorious resurrection on the Last Day.

12. In both of these psalms, the hope is expressed that God will keep believers from going to Sheol.

13. More details are given to us in these passages; details that depict thoughts that usually come to mind when we consider the death of a Christian. Paul says the believer who dies is with Christ. In Luke 23:43, Jesus tells the thief on the cross that he will be with Jesus in paradise after they die.

14. These passages refer to dying as falling asleep, and they call death sleeping. This gives us the tremendous comfort of knowing that, for us, death is not the end—only a time of resting and waiting for the glorious new dawn to come on the day of resurrection.

15. Here we see what it means to "rest in peace." Those who die in the faith no longer struggle against the temptations of the devil, the world, and their sinful nature. They are no longer burdened with temptation or with regret, for those burdens have been taken from them.

Day 4 • 1 Corinthians 15:12–26

16. Believers who are with Christ in heaven await the resurrection of the body on the Last Day. Those who have died are therefore in an interim state rather than their final state.

17. Answers will vary, but will probably include things such as worshiping the Lord. Regardless of what they are doing, we know that those who have departed this life in Christ have been gathered around the presence of God and are existing in perfect joy and contentment. The lecture will consider in some detail what the Bible says about the activities of believers who have died.

18. Answers will vary, but will probably include some of the following: they turn into angels, they are sitting around on clouds playing harps, they look down from heaven and watch over us, or they are reincarnated.

19. Answers will vary, but will probably center on the basic truth given to us in Scripture: the dead in Christ are gathered to the Lord to wait for their glorious resurrection on the Last Day.

Day 5 • Matthew 22:23–33

20. No, Christians do not become angels when they die. An angel is a created spirit; it has no body. A human being without a body is not an angel; he or she is a dead human being. Jesus says that believers will "be *like* the angels." However, this will be "in the resurrection"—that is, after Jesus raises all the dead and gives believers new and glorious bodies. Moreover, believers will be "like the angels" only in the respect that they will not marry or be given in marriage. Jesus is making a specific point about the need for marriage in the age to come, not a general statement about what happens to believers after they die.

21. The Christian's greatest comfort, however, comes from the knowledge that God knows every detail of our lives; "even the hairs of your head are all numbered" (Matthew 10:30). It is worth exploring why some people believe that our deceased loved ones have knowledge of our lives. Perhaps it gives us some comfort.

22. We die because we are sinners. Death came into the world because of sin and, since we are all sinful, death is something that, as long as this present world stands, we will all in time have to pass through.

23. The death of a believer is precious to God. "Are not two sparrows sold for a penny? And not one of them will fall to the ground apart from your Father" (Matthew 10:29). As even the smallest, most insignificant parts of creation are important to God, we know that He will have tremendous regard for the death of His beloved children.

The Justice of God and the Fate of the Wicked, Part 1

Daniel 12:1–3; Matthew 25:31–46; Mark 9:38–50; 2 Thessalonians 1:5–10; Ephesians 2:1–10

Preparing for the Session

Central Focus

On Judgment Day, God will condemn unbelievers to hell, but His judgment is just, because they have rejected His Son despite His attempts to convert them through His Word.

Objectives

That participants, led by the Holy Spirit working through God's Word, will

1. gain an understanding of what will happen on Judgment Day;

2. explain why God is just in condemning some people to hell;

3. describe the terrible torments of hell, based on New Testament passages; and

4. find comfort in the fact that hell was not created for humanity but for the devil and his angels.

For the Small-Group Leader

Small-Group Discussion Helps

Day 1 • Daniel 12:1–3

1. As opposed to those who go to everlasting life, those who end up in everlasting contempt were not wise, nor did they turn others to righteousness.

2. Answers may vary. The Scriptures testify that God's love does not keep Him from sending people to hell, but that He sends people to hell only for lack of faith in Jesus. It is only because He is a loving God that anyone at all is saved from the terrible end.

3. ABSOLUTELY NOTHING! Christians, like unbelievers, deserve to go to hell. We do not earn or deserve to be taken to be with Christ when we die. It is entirely a free gift that God has given us through the life, death, and resurrection of Jesus.

4. Answers will vary, but will probably include descriptions of fire and punishment. The lecture will give more details.

Day 2 • Matthew 25:31–46

5. Here Jesus refers to hell as "the eternal fire." We can be certain that this is hell being described because (a) it is where the wicked go after the judgment, and (b) it is where the devil and his angels will be punished.

6. Those who are cursed by the Father go to hell. We see that they are sent there because they did not care for Jesus when He was in need and they did not care for Jesus by caring for those of His people who were in need.

7. No. Jesus says specifically that hell (the eternal fire) was prepared for the devil and his angels. By contrast, Jesus says that the kingdom inherited by the righteous was prepared for them (v. 34).

8. We are saved by faith apart from works, and passages such as this one should not lead us to doubt that. In reading this text, we can remember that faith always produces good works (such as caring for the needy in the church). Our works flow from, and are a result of, our faith in Christ. We could consider 1 John 4:19: "We love because He first loved us." The lack of good works to which Jesus refers in the parable is evidence of a lack of faith.

9. Answers will vary, and some may express horror at the idea of such terrible, unending punishment. However, we can definitively say that God clearly thinks eternal fire is not too great a punishment, and we believe that God is just.

Day 3 • Mark 9:38–50

10. People who support Jesus' followers when they are persecuted are showing their faith by their works. On the other hand, people who turn away from persecuted believers must ask themselves whether they are not turning away from Jesus!

11. He describes hell as a place where the worm does not die and the fire is not quenched.

12. They refer to hell as a lake of fire and sulfur.

13. He calls it the fiery furnace or the hell of fire.

14. Answers will vary. Some noteworthy information: Sulfur is first mentioned in the Bible in the account of Sodom and Gomorrah (Genesis 19). Its smell was often associated with volcanic activity. When burned, sulfuric gas can harm the lungs, eyes, or other tissues. Hydrogen sulfide, while pungent at first, quickly deadens the sense of smell—so a victim may breathe increasing quantities, which can lead to death.

Day 4 • 2 Thessalonians 1:5–10

15. In this passage, we see people who are being condemned because they persecuted Christians. In these cases, the people's rejection and despising of the Savior turned into hatred toward His people. The outward works of persecution (v. 6), not knowing God, and not obeying the Gospel (v. 8) were a reflection of the inward lack of faith.

16. He says it is eternal destruction and that it is being away from God's presence.

17. He calls it the outer darkness where there is weeping and gnashing of teeth.

18. Clearly from these passages, we can see that the people in hell are in great suffering. The reference to the weeping and gnashing of teeth depicts their agony at being where they are. The reference to the outer darkness shows us that they are separated from the presence of God—they are in the darkness, rather than the light of Christ; and they are left on the outside, rather than being gathered within.

19. Answers will vary. Permit some time for people to share their pictures or descriptions.

Day 5 • Ephesians 2:1–10

20. Answers will vary, but will probably include some of the following: Eternal torment is an unjust punishment for any crime. A loving God would never consign people to torment. Jesus died to save everyone, so no one will go to hell. It is not fair for people to go to hell if they never had a chance to hear about Jesus.

21. Answers will vary. One general line of thought would be this: people go to hell for lack of faith in Jesus. This means that they are condemned for rejecting the one true God.

22. From these passages, we can clearly see that everyone deserves to go to hell—no one deserves to be spared from it.

23. People are delivered from their well-earned condemnation only because God, in His mercy, gave them faith in the atoning sacrifice of Jesus Christ on the cross—not because of their works, but entirely as a gift of God's grace.

24. ABSOLUTELY NOTHING. Even people who end up in heaven deserved to go to hell!

The Justice of God and the Fate of the Wicked, Part 2

Isaiah 1:24–31; Micah 5; Revelation 21:1–8, 22–27; Joel 3:17–21; Daniel 12:1–3

Preparing for the Session

Central Focus

Hell is not simply God's way of punishing unbelievers for ignoring Him; it is also His way of protecting His people from persecution and mistreatment by unbelievers.

Objectives

That participants, led by the Holy Spirit working through God's Word, will

1. explain why God's judgment is just;
2. describe hell as it is portrayed in the Old Testament; and
3. find comfort in the vindication and protection that hell provides for believers.

For the Small-Group Leader

Small-Group Discussion Helps

Day 1 • Isaiah 1:24–31

1. God's intention in this passage is to punish the people who opposed Him and to restore righteousness to Jerusalem.

2. Isaiah 1:29 is a reference to the people falling into the practice of idolatry. It refers to the places of worship and sacrifice to the Canaanite gods.

3. They will burn like dry wood, and no one will be able to quench the fire.

4. It will be redeemed, and it will be called the city of righteousness.

5. These events have not yet taken place. They refer to the Last Day, when the new Jerusalem will come from God in heaven.

Day 2 • Micah 5

6. Israel will be strong enough to defeat the other nations.

7. The children of Abraham are the people who believe in Jesus Christ, so the remnant of Israel in Micah 5:7–8 is us Christians. The descent that God looks at is not whether someone is physically descended from Abraham (i.e., sharing the blood of Abraham), but rather whether someone is of spiritual descent from Abraham (i.e., sharing Abraham's faith in the promised Savior).

8. Regardless of how strong the enemies may seem, in the end, God will defeat them and take vengeance on them.

9. In these passages, God's people have the promise of restoration but are collateral damage as they live among nations that do not obey God. We read that God will destroy their horses and chariots, their fortresses, sorcerers, and idols.

10. The people had put their trust in all the things listed in verses 10–14 instead of fearing, loving, and trusting in God above all things. These verses mean that God will get rid of all idolatry. The temptation to give something else the faith and devotion that we owe to God alone will be forever gone.

Day 3 • Revelation 21:1–8, 22–27

11. Those people who remain faithful until death will live in the holy city Jerusalem. Unbelievers and impenitent people will not live there.

12. These people are left out in part because they are the ones who have tempted and persecuted believers in this life. By keeping them outside the city, God will protect His people from temptation and persecution for all eternity.

13. Gates kept out enemies and defended the city from attack. Since the gates of the holy city Jerusalem will never be shut, that means there are no enemies to threaten the city. We will be completely safe!

14. The comfort is that God will not leave us to the mercy of our enemies forever. He will defend His people and rescue them from their oppressors.

15. Answers may vary. However, the Scriptures draw a clear picture of God's tender concern for His people. He tells us to turn the other cheek and to pray for our persecutors because He wants every human being to repent and be saved. However, He is not willing to let His people be persecuted forever—that would be neither loving nor just. Therefore, at a time He has chosen, He will separate His people from their persecutors and give us eternal protection. "For the LORD will vindicate His people and have compassion on His servants" (Psalm 135:14).

Day 4 • Joel 3:17–21

16. Jerusalem will be holy, and strangers (i.e., people who worship gods besides the one true God) will not come there to tempt, mislead, or persecute God's faithful people.

17. Jesus fulfills the prophecy by creating wine, offering forgiveness, and watering the new Jerusalem with the river of the water of life.

18. They will be desolate because of the innocent blood they shed. Desolation and wilderness imply that thorns and thistles take over the land, and that the population is decimated. Both of these are God's curse against human sin. (See Hosea 10:8.)

19. Judah and Jerusalem will be inhabited forever. Having plenty of wine, milk, and water (v. 18) and having a large population are signs of God's blessing.

Day 5 • Daniel 12:1–3

20. Answers will vary. Allow time for the participants to discuss what they have learned so far.

21. God is love. He sent His Son, Jesus, to atone for the sins of everyone, and He sends the Spirit to work faith in all people through Word and Sacrament. Moreover, out of love for His people, He will finally vindicate us and protect us from the temptations and persecutions of unbelievers.

22. God is just in sending some people to hell. First, we know that, because of our sinfulness, everyone deserves to go to hell. Second, God sends people to hell who have lived without Him. Finally, He sends people to hell to protect His children from the temptations and persecutions of unbelievers.

23. No. The God of the Old Testament and the God of the New Testament are the same God. He calls people to repentance, punishes the impenitent, and gives salvation to believers. Jesus is just as likely to talk about hell and punishment as the Old Testament prophets, and they are just as likely to talk about salvation as Jesus.

24. Answers may vary, but will likely include some of the following: All persecutions will be ended because unbelievers have been separated from us. Since the enemies of God (and therefore the enemies of God's people) have been separated and consigned to hell, the believers in Christ will be safe for all eternity.

The Mercy of God and the Fate of the Redeemed

Revelation 20:11–15; 1 Thessalonians 4:13–18; 1 Corinthians 15:12–28, 35–58; Matthew 25:31–46

Preparing for the Session

Central Focus

On Judgment Day, Jesus will raise both believers and unbelievers from the dead. He will invite believers to inherit the kingdom of God, and He will give them new, glorious, spiritual bodies like His.

Objectives

That participants, led by the Holy Spirit working through God's Word, will

1. distinguish between the resurrection of the dead and the life everlasting;
2. explain what happens to believers on the Last Day; and
3. look forward to the second coming of Jesus with joy.

For the Small-Group Leader

Small-Group Discussion Helps

Day 1 • Revelation 20:11–15

1. Yes, there is a difference; the two phrases, while related to each other, do not refer to exactly the same thing. The bodily resurrection on the Last Day will occur to everyone. Everyone, both believers and unbelievers, will be raised from the dead. However, only believers will enjoy everlasting life.

2. All the dead will be judged, including those who were lost at sea. This implies that all the dead will be raised, but only some will enjoy everlasting life.

3. The word "many" in Daniel 12 means "a large number," or "a multitude" (rather than "most, but not all"). It is a reference to the whole, huge, uncountable mass of humanity. In other words, all the dead will be raised, but only some will enjoy everlasting life.

4. Jesus says that all the dead will be raised, some to the resurrection of judgment and some to the resurrection of life. The resurrection of the body is for everyone, but only believers receive everlasting life.

5. Those whose names were written in the book of life were not thrown into the lake of fire.

Day 2 • 1 Thessalonians 4:13–18

6. Paul's purpose in writing here is to comfort Christians whose loved ones have departed this life in the faith.

7. Believers will rise from the dead, because Jesus Himself died and rose from the dead.

8. Verse 16 says the dead will rise first, and verse 17 says those who are still alive will then be caught up together with them.

9. Believers who are alive are "raptured" along with dead believers when Jesus returns for the final judgment on the Last Day. The *Left Behind* series places the rapture of living believers prior to Jesus' final return and judgment, which is contrary to what is written in verse 17.

10. No, this verse is not talking about a secret rapture prior to Jesus' final return. Paul is writing to comfort believers who have lost Christian loved ones. It is clear that he is talking about Jesus' final return (vv. 16–17), but he is not presenting all there is to say about Jesus' final return. He is focusing on the fate of believers who die before our Lord's second coming.

Day 3 • 1 Corinthians 15:12–28

11. Apparently, some people were saying there is no physical resurrection from the dead. This would mean that people who die before the return of Jesus would not be raised from the dead to enjoy everlasting life.

12. Paul's thinking seems backward to us here: if the dead will not be raised, then Christ was not raised from the dead either. His point is that Christ did not rise from the dead for Himself or His own benefit; Christ rose from the dead in order to give us everlasting life. Therefore, denying the resurrection of Christians is tantamount to denying the resurrection of Christ.

13. Since Christ rose from the dead, and since He rose from the dead in order to give us life, Christians who die before the second coming of Jesus will also rise from the dead.

14. No, it does not mean unbelievers will not be raised from the dead. As with 1 Thessalonians 4, this passage was written to correct a specific false teaching. Paul focuses on the fate of believers rather than listing everything there is to say about Judgment Day.

15. The Sadducees, a party among the Jews, believed there is no resurrection. It is possible that their teaching may have spread into early Christianity, since the first Christians were Jews.

Day 4 • 1 Corinthians 15:35–58

16. With what kind of body are the dead raised? This may have been a loaded question (see v. 36). Just as the Sadducees tried to trap Jesus in Matthew 22:23–33 by making up the story about the woman who married seven brothers, one right after another, so Paul's opponents may have argued that there is no resurrection by questioning what a body would be like in the resurrection.

17. Verses 42–45 state that we will have new, glorious, incorruptible bodies in the resurrection. This is naturally a point of great comfort for Christians, because it means we will no longer suffer from weakness, disease, injury, or death.

18. Answers will vary.

19. In each verse, the word "natural" means opposed to the Spirit of God.

20. In its use here, the word "spiritual" does not mean insubstantial or ethereal, like a ghost or an angel. Rather, a spiritual body is the opposite of the natural body, which is opposed to God's Spirit. The spiritual body is therefore a body that walks in step with the Spirit of God.

Day 5 • Matthew 25:31–46

21. When Jesus says, "Come," He is going to provide His wonderful blessings to the people He is inviting.

22. You inherit because of your relationship to a person or because someone writes you into his or her will. It is not your action, but the other person's action. Therefore, when we receive the kingdom of heaven, it is not by our action but by God's action.

23. God prepared the kingdom for believers before the world was created.

24. No. The works Jesus points out are simply evidence of faith.

25. ABSOLUTELY NOTHING! They enter heaven because God had blessed them with faith.

"Behold, the Dwelling Place of God Is with Man"

2 Peter 3:1–13; Revelation 21; Isaiah 11:1–9; Luke 20:27–40; Revelation 21:1–8

Preparing for the Session

Central Focus

When we talk about eternal life, we tend to talk about going to heaven. The Scriptures, however, reveal a far richer picture of everlasting life. Our gracious Father will create new, perfect heavens and earth for believers, and He will live in that new creation with us forever.

Objectives

That participants, led by the Holy Spirit working through God's Word, will

1. understand the biblical concept of the new heavens and the new earth;
2. rejoice in the knowledge that God will dwell with His people; and
3. find courage and encouragement in the glory to come.

For the Small-Group Leader

Small-Group Discussion Helps

Day 1 • 2 Peter 3:1–13

1. Jesus is slow only by our definition. He is putting off His second coming to give as many people as possible the opportunity to repent and believe in Him.

2. "Heavens" in verse 7 does not refer to the dwelling place of God but rather to the firmament of the sky, which is a part of this sinful creation.

3. We read here that creation (i.e., this present world) will be destroyed by fire.

4. Verse 13 states, "According to His promise we are waiting for new heavens and a new earth in which righteousness dwells." In other words, God has promised to make a new creation for us to live in following the Last Day.

5. Answers will vary, but may include the following: We can find comfort in this by seeing that although this present world is fallen, troubled, and corrupt, we know that on the Last Day it will be gone forever and replaced with a new creation that will be perfect and unsullied by sin.

Day 2 • Revelation 21

6. After the Judgment Day, believers will live in their resurrected bodies in the new heavens and the new earth.

7. God will also live in the new heavens and the new earth, with His redeemed people.

8. The answer depends on what we mean by the word "heaven." If by heaven a person means in the presence of God, then yes, it is correct to say that we will live in heaven forever. However, if by heaven a person means the uncreated realm of God (as if we float about without bodies, playing harps), then no. Also, if a person describes heaven as a recreated earth but makes no reference to our direct communion with God and the Lamb, then no. What the Scriptures say is that we will live on the new earth, and God will live with us.

9. Revelation 7:14 says it best when it describes those who are gathered around the throne of God: "These are the ones coming out of the great tribulation. They have washed their robes and made them white in the blood of the Lamb." Through faith in Christ, our sins have been washed away. We are confident in what Jesus has done for us.

10. We are offered amazing promises. "He will wipe away every tear from their eyes, and death shall be no more, neither shall there be mourning, nor crying, nor pain anymore, for the former things have passed away" (v. 4).

Day 3 • Isaiah 11:1–9

11. Jesse was the father of King David. The shoot from the stump of Jesse is Jesus. Isaiah uses the imagery of a stump to point out that the sons of David, who ruled from about 1000 BC, would be cut off by 586 BC. You could say that David's royal family tree would be chopped down. However, because of God's promise to send a Savior through David, a shoot would grow from the stump.

12. Jesus' rule will differ from all those who reigned previously. He will rule with perfect justice, equity, and righteousness.

13. These verses are clearly describing for us the messianic age—that is, the time when Jesus comes back and reverses the order of sinful creation. After the Last Day, creation will once again be like Eden.

14. Peace throughout all of creation will be grounded in the knowledge of the Lord, which will be worldwide.

15. Since we still worry if our children go off into the woods alone, this must be describing a future state of affairs. It is a description of everlasting life.

Day 4 • Luke 20:27–40

16. Answers will vary.

17. No, it does not. As we have already seen, this passage is talking about life "in the resurrection"—that is, after Jesus' second coming. Moreover, Jesus says we will be like the angels in one respect, not that we will be like the angels in every way. An angel without a body is an angel, but a human being without a body is dead.

18. Answers will vary. A nice, short answer is that God's command to be fruitful and multiply was given to humanity for this creation. Marriage is God's institution within which we fulfill that command. The reasons include the fact that marriage was fulfilled in Christ (Ephesians 5:22–33).

19. Answers will vary.

20. Answers will vary. The point is that we, as God's people, will be wed to the Lamb, Jesus Christ.

Day 5 • Revelation 21:1–8

21. Answers will vary.

22. He is promising to bring them back from their punishment in captivity by giving them a heart to know that He is the Lord; to do away with their present suffering with His loving covenant; and to protect them forever as their loving God and Father.

23. No. God makes Himself their God by cleansing them from their idolatry.

24. After God says that He will be their God, the people turn away from all their idols to worship and serve the one true God faithfully.

25. God will completely cleanse us from our sins through the blood of Jesus. He has already taken away our punishment through the death of Jesus, and He will do away with our suffering and protect us forever. We will therefore serve the true God faithfully.

"And They Will Be His People"

Psalm 16; Romans 7:12–25; Isaiah 25:6–12; 60; Revelation 21:1–7

Preparing for the Session

Central Focus

Our idea of heaven often reflects what we most love in this life. Thankfully, what heaven is like will not be decided by our desires, but by God in His grace and goodness. In heaven, we will have everything we want, and we will want only what God has given us.

Objectives

That participants, led by the Holy Spirit working through God's Word, will

1. describe how our earthly desires often color our ideas about heaven;
2. understand the relationship between the new creation and God's Law;
3. overcome worries about boredom in heaven; and
4. look forward to a time when our desires are in line with God's gifts.

For the Small-Group Leader

Small-Group Discussion Helps

Day 1 • Psalm 16

1. We will have pleasures at the right hand of God forevermore.

2. Answers will vary. Common perceptions include ideas such as being able to do whatever we want: if something brings us pleasure in this life, then surely we will have an abundance of it in the next. A fisherman might assume he will spend eternity fishing on the perfect lake, a preteen may assume heaven will be full of video games, and so forth.

3. Answers will vary, but most will probably not find much support for the above ideas in this Psalm. The joy being expressed in Psalm 16 is that God will not abandon our souls to Sheol but will deliver us to Himself. In His presence, we will find true joy and contentment forever. In other words, our joy is in being saved from what we by our sins have deserved and being permitted to bask in the glory of the radiance of God. There is no reference here to being able to do whatever we want or that earthly pleasures will exist for us there.

4. Answers will vary. Give participants time to discuss their thoughts.

Day 2 • Romans 7:12–25

5. Although at times we may not want to hear it, we know that the Law of God is always good. Sometimes it makes us feel bad, but the Law is from God and is therefore good.

6. As Paul makes clear, sin is active in our natural bodies. Our desires do not always line up with the Law.

7. These texts show us that, contrary to what we may ordinarily assume, our desires are not pure at all. As with every other part of us, our desires have been corrupted by our sinful nature.

8. What we like in this life might well be sinful (take, for example, the case of the Muslim idea of heaven). Heaven is not something that is formed around our desires but rather around the majesty and glory of the presence of God.

9. Answers will vary, but participants will probably form their responses around the promises God has made to us about heaven in His Word. A wise old pastor used to say, "You will do what your heart wants to do when you get there."

For reference: According to Muslim teachings, each Muslim man who gets to heaven will have seventy-two virgins with whom he can have sex whenever he wants. The women will remain virgins, even after he has been with them. Also, little boys will cater an ongoing feast for the man.

Day 3 • Isaiah 25:6–12

10. Here heaven is described with the image of a great feast.

11. These passages depict heaven as a wedding feast.

12. We tend to eat when we gather socially (e.g., "Why don't you come over for burgers?" you say to your neighbors on the Fourth of July). Eating together can be as much about social life as about nourishing the body. People in Bible times understood feasting in this way: it was not simply about nourishing the body at the same time but about enjoying communion with one another.

13. Feasting with God means enjoying communion with Him.

14. In each passage, God (or the character representing God, in the case of parables) gives the feast. He is the one who invites. This means that our communion with God in heaven flows from His divine invitation rather than from our action. He establishes our communion (or relationship) with Him, and He sustains it.

Day 4 • Isaiah 60

15. The nations will come to the holy city and bring their wealth in—their sheep and camels, their silver and gold, their fine lumber.

16. Camels carried goods, and flocks of sheep and goats were a form of wealth in the ancient world, just as large herds of cattle are a form of wealth in many Midwestern and Western states of our nation.

17. The city gates remain open so the nations can bring their wealth in.

18. a. The holy city Jerusalem will provide light for the nations (Isaiah 60:3; Revelation 21:24).

b. Sun and moon will be unnecessary, because the Lord will be the light of the city (Isaiah 60:19–20; Revelation 21:23).

c. The nations and kings will bring their glory into the city (Isaiah 60:5–13; Revelation 21:24, 26).

d. The gates of the city will never be shut (Isaiah 60:11; Revelation 21:25).

e. The city will be perfectly safe from sin and sinners (Isaiah 60:18; Revelation 21:27).

19. These passages and others like them suggest that there will be massive offerings to the Lord in heaven. It is difficult to know whether to take the passages literally. Even if they are to be taken literally, we must be careful not to understand offerings in the context of our lives in this age. If offerings to the Lord are a sign of dedication to the Lord (as in Isaiah 19:21), then these images may be a way of saying that everyone from every nation will be fully devoted to the Lord in the age to come.

Day 5 • Revelation 21:1–7

20. The three parts of God's promise in this text are that God will dwell with humanity, that He will be our God, and that we will be His people.

21. Being God's people means that they will be wholly devoted to Him (unlike their past lives of unfaithfulness).

22. God's Law will be in their hearts, and they will all know God rightly.

23. The spiritual body is a physical body that follows the promptings of the Spirit; the natural body is a physical body that fights against the Spirit.

24. Our desires in this life are still sinful. Our desires in the life to come will be fully in step with the Spirit and with the Law of God. We will be His people, wholly devoted to Him.

"For the Healing of the Nations"

Genesis 4:1–16; 11:1–9; Matthew 8:5–13; Ephesians 2:11–16; Isaiah 2:2–5

Preparing for the Session

Central Focus

Life in this age is filled with conflict, but in the new heavens and the new earth, we will enjoy perfect peace, because the tree of life will grow there, and "the leaves of the tree were for the healing of the nations" (Revelation 22:2).

Objectives

That participants, led by the Holy Spirit working through God's Word, will

1. understand conflict (interpersonal and international) as a symptom of human sinfulness;

2. seek reconciliation in the power of the Spirit; 3. rejoice in the great diversity of the Church on earth; and

4. look with longing for the perfect peace of the age to come.

For the Small-Group Leader

Small-Group Discussion Helps

Day 1 • Genesis 4:1–16

1. Answers will vary, but as we see in our passage, envy and resentfulness can easily simmer, fester, and explode into an outward conflict.

2. Answers may vary. The root cause seems to have been anger that Abel's sacrifice was accepted. The anger may have flowed from jealousy.

3. Cain murdered his brother because his deeds were evil but Abel's were righteous.

4. Cain did not offer his sacrifice correctly. The Hebrews text reminds us that without faith, it is impossible to please God. First John 3:12 clearly notes that he was "of the evil one". Apparently Cain was without a faith relationship with God.

5. "We love because He first loved us" (1 John 4:19). As people who have been reconciled to God through Christ, we set aside our own anger and jealousy in order to seek reconciliation with people around us.

Day 2 • Genesis 11:1–9

6. Answers will vary.

7. Because the people were still all gathered together in one group, the only one they could possibly have been trying to show off in front of was God. They were trying to make a name for themselves with God!

8. The people were showing pride, as if they could elevate themselves from earth to heaven and sit next to God and make a name for themselves with Him.

9. The divisions among peoples occurred because God confused the language of humanity at Babel and then scattered the people across the earth to prevent them from again uniting to attempt what they were doing in Babel.

10. Unfortunately, after the fall of the tower, the people's attitude of pride did not go away. It still shows itself today in each group's thinking that it is superior to others or that it deserves special privileges.

Day 3 • Matthew 8:5–13

11. Most Jews would have looked on him with suspicion because (a) he was a Gentile, (b) he was an instrument of Roman rule, and (c) Roman soldiers did not usually treat the people of the land particularly well.

12. Jesus was amazed to see such faith in a Gentile when He had not seen it among His own people, the people of Israel.

13. The "sons of the kingdom" are Jews who reject Jesus (not all Jews, just those who reject Jesus).

14. People from east and west—that is, Gentiles like this centurion! This idea would have been offensive to many Jews in Jesus' day, because they believed that the Gentiles would serve the Jews in the age to come. Jesus is basically saying that the unbelieving Jews would not sit with their own patriarchs, while believing Gentiles would.

15. Answers will vary, but the main point is that He came to save both Jews and Gentiles, and in heaven people of all nations will sit at one table in communion with God.

Day 4 • Ephesians 2:11–16

16. The Gentile Christians were at one time outside God's promise to Abraham and therefore outside of salvation. This is difficult for us Gentiles to understand, but Paul's point is that God's promise of salvation was made to Abraham and his descendants. Gentiles, like us, are saved only by becoming children of Abraham through faith in Christ.

17. The two being referred to are the believing Jews and believing Gentiles—we are one through our faith in Christ Jesus.

18. The two now one should relate to each other in love, not hostility. After all, they are brothers and sisters in Christ.

19. Peter acted as if there were still a division between Jews and Gentiles, when he knew from his vision in Acts 10 that our Lord Jesus had overcome the dividing wall of hostility.

20. In Christ Jesus, all the divisions among us have been overcome. In Christ, we are one people despite coming from various tribes, languages, peoples, and nations.

Day 5 • Isaiah 2:2–5

21. All nations and many people shall come and learn from the Lord.

22. Being in perfect communion with God means that the nations will enjoy perfect peace with one another instead of warfare and strife.

23. The leaves of the tree of life in Revelation 22:1–2 bring about "healing of the nations," which is what Isaiah 2:2–5 is talking about.

24. Answers will vary, but should reflect the concept of believers of all nations joining together in the peace of Christ.

25. People of every nation, tribe, people, and language will join their voices together in one heavenly chorus to God in the age to come. The Church can and should show the world that our confession of Jesus Christ as the Lamb who was slain overcomes every racial and ethnic division in this life.

Living Heavenward

Genesis 1:26–31; Exodus 20:8–11; Deuteronomy 5:12–15; 1 Peter 3:13–22; Luke 21:29–36; Revelation 22

Preparing for the Session

Central Focus

The hope of heaven does not draw our attention away from this life. Rather, it sustains us in this life and moves us to share the Good News with others so they may also enjoy everlasting life with God.

Objectives

That participants, led by the Holy Spirit working through God's Word, will

1. embrace their earthly vocations as signs of God's love toward the world;
2. seek to prefigure the peace of heaven in their relationships;
3. learn to live in hope of the age to come; and
4. develop strategies to share the good news of heaven with others.

For the Small-Group Leader

Small-Group Discussion Helps

Day 1 • Genesis 1:26–31

1. God commanded Adam and Eve to fill the earth and subdue it.

2. Adam and Eve worshiped the Lord by doing what God commanded them to do: being fruitful and multiplying, filling the earth and subduing it, and rulin over the creatures God created.

3. Adam's vocation was to care for the garden, to work and keep it.

4. The various jobs all fit into God's command to fill the earth and subdue it and to care for this creation. We serve God and our fellow human beings by doing these jobs.

5. Many people feel a tension, as if time spent in daily work is time away from communion with God, or as if ordinary work is a necessary evil. Nothing could be further from the truth. Genesis 1 and 2 show us that work is form of worship, because God created us to care for this creation.

Day 2 • Exodus 20:8–11; Deuteronomy 5:12–15

6. The Sabbath was to be kept by refraining from work.

7. According to Exodus, the people are to observe the Sabbath because God Himself rested on the seventh day from His work of creating. According to Deuteronomy, it is to remember God's great act of deliverance when He brought the people out of Egypt.

8. "You shall not do any work but shall worship the Lord in His temple, day and night"—or something along those lines.

9. God wants us to rest because we can take the good gift of work and turn it into an idol. God therefore reminds us to stop working in order to hear His Word. Doing so is a sign of trust that He will provide for us.

10. The Third Commandment reminds us not to make work our idol, but the mandate in Genesis 1 and 2 reminds us not to use worship as an excuse to neglect everyday work for what we assume to be more spiritual pursuits.

Day 3 • 1 Peter 3:13–22

11. In times of persecution, we are called to suffer patiently and use the opportunity to explain why we do so.

12. We are pointed to the hope of everlasting life, which we have through Jesus Christ, our Savior.

13. Answers will vary. Our hope is certainly a fruit of faith in Christ, and faith trusts the Lord to bring our sufferings to an end and give us eternal glory.

14. Answers will vary.

15. We are always strengthened when we hear the promises of God in the Scriptures and in preaching, and we find support from fellow Christians.

Day 4 • Luke 21:29–36

16. We should watch so that we are not caught in sin and unfaithfulness at His second coming.

17. Thoughts of Jesus' second coming should encourage Christians to remain faithful so that we escape the judgment coming on the world.

18. In Luke 21:25–28, the promise of our Lord's return gives us comfort, because it means our redemption from the suffering of this world.

19. Knowing that we have life eternal in Christ sustains us even during our most difficult times, such as when we suffer.

20. Thoughts of heaven should not keep us from our earthly work of caring for other people. When we think about heaven, we do so knowing that the Lord Jesus will return to judge the living and the dead. This encourages us not to grow slack in our Christian faith or in our vocations. At the same time, we are sustained through the difficulties and sufferings of this world by the knowledge that our Lord will one day return to redeem us from them.

Day 5 • Revelation 22

21. The purpose of this chapter appears to be to give comfort to the recipients with the knowledge that Jesus is coming back soon.

22. The Spirit and the Church cry out for the Lord Jesus to come back, because our Lord's return spells the end of suffering and the beginning of life in the age to come.

23. Jesus promises three times that He is coming soon. The promise is repeated to give us hope in the midst of our suffering.

24. Answers will vary. The reality is that eternal life is ours through Christ Jesus alone.

25. Answers will vary. Take time to pray for those who don't know the hope that is in Christ and for the strength and words to share that hope with those who need to hear it.